DAIJIRO KATO

First published in Japanese by Kodansha Publishing Co. Ltd

This English-language edition published in 2006 by
Haynes Publishing, Sparkford,
Yeovil, Somerset, BA22 7JJ, UK
Tel: 01963 442030 Fax: 01963 440001
Int. tel: +44 1963 442030 Int. fax: +44 1963 440001
E-mail: sales@haynes.co.uk
Website: www.haynes.co.uk

This product is officially licensed by Dorna SL, owners of the MotoGP trademark (© Dorna 2006)

A catalogue record for this book is available from the British Library

ISBN 1 84425 358 9

Library of Congress catalog card no. 2006928052

Haynes North America, Inc.,
861 Lawrence Drive, Newbury Park,
California 91320, USA

Printed and bound in England by
J. H. Haynes & Co. Ltd, Sparkford

Contents

Prologue – A piece of the puzzle   6
Takashi Kato (Daijiro's father)   10
Hatsumi Kato (Daijiro's mother)   14

2000/2001 The road to the 250cc World Championship   **20**
Fausto Gresini (Manager of Team Gresini)   22
Fabrizio Cecchini (Mechanic with Team Gresini)   23
Hitoshi Tagawa (Mechanic with Team Gresini)   26
Shinya Nakano (MotoGP racer)   30
Marco Melandri (MotoGP racer)   34
Michela Fabbri (Team Gresini press officer)   35
Tetsuya Harada (ex-250cc World Champion)   38

MotoGP 2002 NSR500/RC211V   **40**
Mick Doohan (ex-500CC World Champion)   42
Max Biaggi (MotoGP racer)   43
Teruaki Matsubara (HRC engineer)   46
Kazuto Sakata (ex-125cc World Champion)   47
Noboru Ueda (ex-125cc GP racer)   50
Youichi Ui (Grand Prix racer)   51
Akiro Ryo (Suzuki works rider)   54
Hikaru Miyagi (ex-HRC racer)   55
Kenny Roberts Snr (ex-500cc World Champion)   62

1976 - 1993 From Akigase to the Kyushu Championship   **64**
Tomomi Motoyama (Daijiro's pocket bike coach)   66
Makoto Takeda (a pocket bike and mini bike friend)   67
Kazunori Bito (owner of BRD)   70
Tokuo Iobe (owner of I-Factory)   74
Mitsuo Abe (Norifumi Abe's father and a Japanese speedway racer)   75
Fukumi Kotake (Manager of Team Kotake)   78

1994 - 1999 Glory and frustration 80

Shinichi Ito (ex-Grand Prix racer) 82
Yukio Kagayama (British and World Superbike Championship racer) 83
Noriyasu Numata (ex All Japan 250cc Champion) 87
Takahiro Sohwa (ex-All Japan Championship racer) 90
Naoki Matsudo (250cc Grand Prix racer) 94
Toshiyuki Yamaji (HRC engineer) 98
Yukiharu Kiyota (HRC engineer) 102

1994 – 2002 Suzuka Eight Hour races 104

Shinya Takeishi (ex-All Japan Championship Superbike racer) 106
Takuma Aoki (ex-Grand Prix racer) 107
Kunimitsu Takahashi (ex-Grand Prix racer) 110
Tohru Ukawa (MotoGP racer) 111
Hitoyasu Izutsu (ex-All Japan Superbike Champion) 114
Alex Baros (MotoGP racer) 115
Colin Edwards (MotoGP racer) 118
Tomohiro Hasegawa (Shoei Helmet) 119
Tadahiko Taira (ex-Grand Prix racer) 122
Manabu Kamata (HRC test rider) 126

2003 The Japanese GP: lap 3 128

Kiyoshi Kawashima (supreme advisor at Honda Motor Co Ltd) 130
Takeo Fukui (President and CEO of Honda Motor Co Ltd) 131
Suguru Kanazawa (President of HRC) 134
Shoji Tachikawa (HRC Repsol Honda team manager) 135
Tadayuki Okada (ex-HRC racer and former assistant manager of
the GP team) 138
Loris Capirossi (ex-125cc and 250cc World Champion and
MotoGP racer) 139
Ryoichi Mori (mechanic with Team Gresini) 142
Valentino Rossi (MotoGP and 500cc World Champion) 146
Takashi Kamata (sports trainer) 147
Nobuatsu Aoki (MotoGP racer) 150
Carlo Merlini (Team Gresini staff member) 151
Sete Gibernau (MotoGP racer) 154

'Daijiro, we miss you'   **160**
Michael Scott (British motorcycle journalist)   162
Iain Mackay (Honda press officer)   163
Satoshi Endo (GP journalist)   166
Hidenobu Takeuchi (GP photographer)   170
Mat Oxley (British freelance journalist)   171
Manuel Pecino (Spanish journalist)   174
Stefano Saragoni (Moto Sprint magazine – Italy)   175
Shigeo Kibiki (GP photographer)   179
Jun Aoki (Chief Editor of Riding Sports)   182
Takanao Tsubouchi (Head of Vega International)   183
Tsuyoshi Chiwa (Associate Editor of Moto Champ magazine)   186

2003 – Wins dedicated to Daijiro   **188**
Norifumi Abe (MotoGP racer)   190
Shingo Yanagimoto (Daijiro's mechanic and personal manager)   194
Makoto Tamada (MotoGP racer)   198
Haruchika Aoki (ex-125cc World Champion)   202
Noriyuki Haga (World Superbike Championship racer)   206
Katsuaki Fujiwara (Supersport World Championship racer)   207
Naoki Hattori (car racer)   210
Satoshi Tsujimoto (ex-All Japan racer)   214
Junko Yamashita (Daijiro's team co-ordinator)   218
Chojun Kameya (All Japan Championship racer and Daijiro's cousin)   222
Yuichi Takeda (rider and driver)   226
Satoshi Motoyama (All Japan GT and Forumula Nippon
  Championship driver)   230
Makiko Kato (Daijiro's wife)   234
Hiromi Sato (motorcycle journalist)   246
Yoko Tagashi (motorcycle journalist)   250

Words from Daijiro   254

Epilogue   256

Race results   258

Daijiro moved up to the MotoGP class in 2002 but was riding the two-stroke NSR500 for the first half of the season. *(Team Gresini)*

Prologue

A piece of the puzzle

On 18 May 2003, nearly ten thousand fans gathered for the 'Farewell Daijiro Kato Ceremony' which was held at Honda Motor headquarters in Tokyo.

The long queue of fans, who were waiting to get into the building, snaked for several kilometres away from Honda headquarters. A guard holding a sign that said 'the end of the queue' was telling them that they would have to wait for two-and-a-half hours before getting in. Still, they all waited outside without complaining, in order to say goodbye to their hero, Daijiro. They wanted to say 'Thank you' and 'Goodbye', and they also wanted to say how much they missed him, how sorry they were to lose him, and how much they had expected of him. They waited and waited, and it was like a waiting room where they could get themselves ready to confront reality, the death of Daijiro.

After saying 'Goodbye' to Daijiro, I got on the metro from Aoyama Icchome station. A beautiful girl in her late twenties sat in front of me. She took a white envelope out of her bag which had been presented at the 'Farewell Daijiro Kato Ceremony'. Three photos of Daijiro, a sticker and a message card from Honda were inside the envelope. The message said: 'Thank you Dai-chan. We will never forget your fighting spirit.'

Hesitating slightly, the girl took the photographs out of the envelope, looked admiringly at each of them for a while and then, as the train was approaching the next station, she put them back into the envelope. I saw a tear rolling down her cheek: another of Daijiro's fans who would shed lonely tears. She wanted nobody to see her tears and she wanted to say farewell to her hero on her own.

On the day Daijiro passed away, fans all over the world mourned . They were sorry for Daijiro's family, and sad for the sport and for themselves.

After the dreadful accident at Suzuka many people had spent sleepless nights, praying for God to bring him back to life, but it did not happen. Miracle was merely a word in the dictionary. Daijiro passed away on 20 April, after two weeks of fighting his last fight.

Then came the day when we had to say goodbye to Daijiro. There were many fans outside the temple. When the car with Daijiro's body inside sounded its horn before leaving the temple for the crematorium, many fans cried, screamed and called Daijiro's name. There were also many fans clapping their hands. Rather unusual, you may think – but they were clapping the champion, clapping hands for their hero. While they clapped they were watching the clouds floating up in the sky, tears still falling down their cheeks.

Everybody misses him. Everyone feels a large hollow inside, a hollow which can never be filled. A year has already passed since that time, but our tears never dry.

Daijiro Kato, a rider of genius who was eager to win the MotoGP Championship, had two faces. One was the face of a lonely fighter who had to do battle in the tough world of motorcycle racing. The other face of Daijiro was that of a family man, a husband and father who enjoyed a warm and gentle life with those closest to him.

In both worlds there are many people who supported and lived with him. They all have a piece of the puzzle in their heart: the puzzle of Daijiro. We have asked them to share these pieces, their precious memories of Daijiro.

Everybody in this book kindly described their particular pieces. The last piece is the one you have in your heart: if you can find your piece of the puzzle, you can read this book with your own heart-warming memories of Daijiro.

My friend Hiromi Sato and I asked 74 people for their comments. When we explained about the book and asked them for their help, not one refused. Even the busy guys, like Valentino Rossi and Max Biaggi, were eager to help and co-operate with us. This is all because of Daijiro. Everybody loved him.

Of course, there are many more people whom we did not have the chance to ask for their comments. In this book, the thoughts of those who are not listed are also included.

Luckily, as motorcycle journalists, we had many opportunities to talk to Daijiro and, as we put the book together, we discovered that we were two of Daijiro Kato's most enthusiastic fans.

Yoko Togashi
March 2004

Before the start of the 2003 season, Daijiro said his aim was to win his first MotoGP race as soon as possible. *(Team Gresini)*

OPPOSITE PAGE: On April 6, 2003, Daijiro lined up at the grid. 'He was calm and serene' said his mechanic, Ryoichi Mori. *(Team Gresini)*

Takashi Kato

Daijiro's father

I wish he could have won a race on the RC211V

Daijiro was a long-awaited child. He was born five years after we married, and he was the apple of our eyes. Hoping that he would grow up in good health, we made him do various sports like swimming, skiing and Kenseido (a martial art) for exercise in his childhood. Initially he hated doing all these things.

It was just before Daijiro was three that we encountered pocket bikes. I was walking around a department store with my wife and saw a black pocket bike displayed in the window. It looked really interesting and I bought it on the spot as a present for his third birthday. At first he cried from fear every time I started the engine, so he used to push the bike around with his feet, with the engine off. About a year later I put a stopper on the throttle so that he could ride slowly with the engine idling, and then altered it little by little so he could get used to the speed.

I started my own transport company just after he was born – only one small truck – and used to be away from home occasionally. 'You are a boy so you must defend your mom while I'm gone,' I would say to him before I left. He was about four years old, but he nodded in agreement. I'd sometimes taken him with me to work when he was younger – I was given his diapers by my wife, and we'd go to my work nearby.

Daijiro started pocket bike racing at Akigase, and then moved up to mini bikes. Afterwards I hoped he would take a title in the All Japan Championship. I used to go along with him wherever he went, but one day he said, 'Can you stay out of my racing from now on?' That was when he was in high school and had joined Team Kotake. 'I'll take care of myself,' he added. He seemed more independent, and I was glad rather than sad to hear that. After that I just watched him from a distance, even when I went to the track. I rarely went to the paddock to visit him.

I was watching a monitor in his team suite during the Japanese GP, and didn't realise immediately from the scene of the accident that it was him. When I heard that it was Daijiro I rushed to the medical centre. He was then transferred to a hospital in Yokkaichi where he was confirmed as brain dead. For two weeks I kept saying, 'Hang in there!' but he couldn't survive.

I never thought that would happen. I was hoping he would quit racing at the age of about 33 and then do whatever he wanted. I didn't believe he would suffer an accident before that age, because it was then that many riders, like Wayne Rainey or Mick Doohan, had got seriously injured. I also wish he could have won at least one race on the RC211V, because he was training harder than ever and had committed himself to the season.

I went to Italy in June to pack up the stuff at his apartment. 'Everyone in Misano was a fan of Daijiro's,' the Mayor of Misano said when we visited the town hall. They love motorcycles there, and had accepted him as one of their own. Daijiro was hoping motorcycles would become more popular in Japan again too, that's why he started the Daijiro Cup, to offer opportunities for as many children as possible to ride pocket bikes. I think I will continue to run the Daijiro Cup for him, and if the idea could spread worldwide he would be happy.

In 2003 Daijiro started a pocket bike series, the Daijiro Cup: the pre-event press call. *(Daijiro.net)*

ABOVE: Daijiro and his father, Takashi Kato. *(Takashi Kato)*

OPPOSITE: Daijiro was Takashi and Hatsumi Kato's long-awaited only child. *(Takashi Kato)*

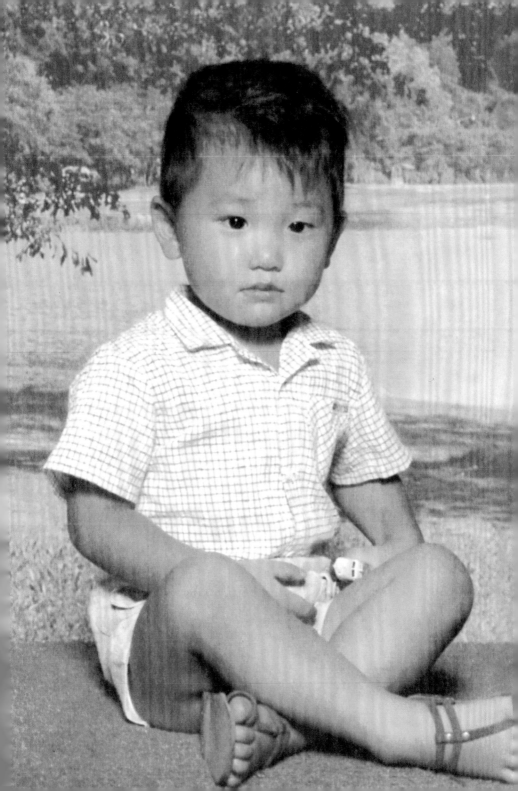

Hatsumi Kato

Daijiro's mother

Dai-chan did not like to be alone

When Dai-chan was born he weighed only 2.4kg, but his grandmother said he had a very good grip the first time she took care of him and gave him a bath. 'This baby is so strong!' she said, and reassured me that he was a bouncing, healthy boy. However, he used to want all the lights on in the house – he was an only child and did not like to be alone when it was dark and quiet.

Dai-chan liked to spend time with lots of friends, and he was always saying to visitors 'Come on in, come on in!' or 'Stay at my house overnight, do stay at my house!' Almost every weekend, when he was racing pocket bikes and mini bikes, friends such as Yu-chan (Yuichi Takeda) and Nori (Norifumi Abe) would stay. Usually several boys, maybe five or six of them, would come over with no change of clothes, so they used Dai-chan's clothes. Even underwear, too.

In the days of pocket bike racing, all the families would go to the circuit. There were no facilities for buying food so we mothers made plans, deciding who would prepare rice balls for the kids and whose turn it was to make Ton-Jiru (pork miso soup).

Even during the holidays we went to the circuit. We never took him to Disneyland and other places where kids went. Racing was top priority; he even attended the school's yearly athletic meeting only once.

After school finished on a Friday we waited for him at the school gate and took him directly to the circuit. We needed to be there before classes ended, otherwise he would go off to play with friends! One day he did not come out, so I asked his class-mate where he was, and he said 'Dai-chan? He was scolded by a teacher again and told to stand in the hall.' There was one time when I could hear the teacher yelling at him in the halls. He was always up to mischief, and he liked to joke around.

When he rode the pocket bike I was not afraid to watch, but I became nervous when he stepped up to the mini bike class. Thirty minutes before the race my heart was beating so fast that I could hear it myself. When I did watch I had to cover my mouth, as I might have screamed with fright. But when the race finished and he ended up second, I used to ask him, 'Were you racing? Or were you just "touring around"?' We expected him to win and he was not rewarded even when he won a race. Maybe I was too hard on him. In addition, I did not let him make excuses. When he tried that I would say to him, 'No excuses!'

During his high school period he was taken care of by Team Kotake in Kyushu. Every Saturday morning we took him to Haneda national airport – he would be on his own, carrying a helmet and his leathers – and he came back by the last flight on Sunday. We never allowed him to be absent from school, though. We thought that it would become a habit for him not to go if once we agreed, although it seems he did sleep at his desk. His teacher said, 'It was not really sleeping, he was just good at taking power naps!'

We went to watch the Japanese GP at Suzuka in 2000, the year he started to take part in the World Championship. I was very relieved when Dai-chan was well liked by everyone, including Mr Gresini. I thought that the team was really family orientated and very nice.

I was so happy, too, when he introduced Makiko and talked about his plans to take her to Europe with him, because I was expecting him to get married soon. I was also excited and happy when I got news from him that she was pregnant. I was confident that Dai-chan would stick to his work, even after having a child. After Ikko was born, he started to call us more frequently. I think he began to understand things from a parent's perspective.

On that day, at Suzuka, we were taking care of Ikko in the team suite while Dai-chan was on the track. Before the start of the race, Dai-chan left the suite, saying, 'I am going now.' Everything was normal.

During the race, I did not realise at once from the TV who had crashed. It was only my husband who went to the medical centre soon after the accident. Some time after that, Shingo-san (Dai-chan's personal manager) came to me and said: 'You'd better come as well…'

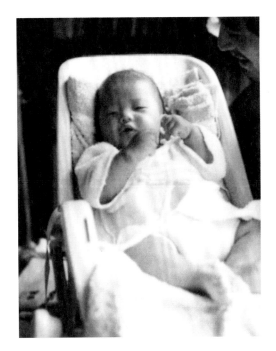

Daijiro was born on 4 July 1976, a small (2.4kg) but healthy baby.
(Takashi Kato)

Daijiro and his mother, Hatsumi.
(Takashi Kato)

Daijiro's parents let him try various sports, including Kenseido. *(Takashi Kato)*

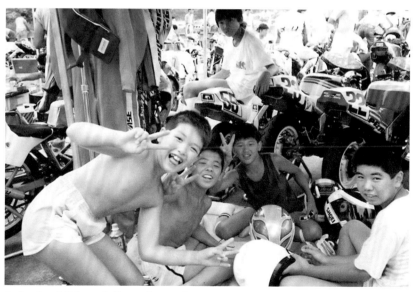

During the mini bike era Daijiro made many friends. *From left* Yuichi Takeda, Chojun Kameya, Daijiro, with Norick Abe sitting behind. *(Takashi Kato)*

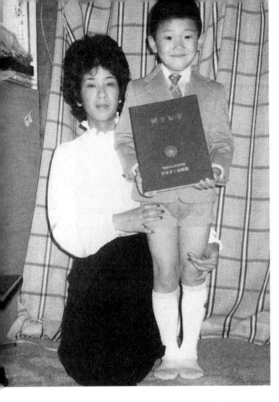

18 Daijiro Kato

2000–2001

The road to the 250cc World Championship

Daijiro started to take part in the GPs as a regular racer in 2000. In the 250cc class that year there were three Japanese riders fighting for the title – Tohru Ukawa (Honda), who had been racing in the class since '96, Shinya Nakano (Yamaha), who had joined the 250cc class the previous year, and Daijiro, the rookie. Daijiro won the third round, at Suzuka, but could not repeat his first-place finish until the Portuguese GP, in the latter half of the season. Then, after winning in Portugal, Daijiro won the Rio GP and the Pacific GP (at Motegi) consecutively, finishing third in the championship behind the French rider, Olivier Jacque (Yamaha) and Nakano.

In 2001 Daijiro led the championship from the start of the season, but he had a strong rival that year. Tetsuya Harada, who'd won the 250cc championship in '93 on a Yamaha, came back to the class after riding an Aprilia 500cc machine for the previous two years. Harada was six years older than Daijiro but was eager to confront his super-strong rival.

Daijiro won the opening round at Suzuka, bringing Honda close to its 500th GP win. He went on to win the next three races, but Harada was consistent in his riding too and got on the podium in every one of those races. Then Harada won the fifth round, in Italy, and was catching up with Daijiro. Round 6, in Catalunya, was the highlight of the season. In their fierce battle Kato and Harada fought at the very peak of road racing, with Daijiro staying behind Tetsuya at the start in order to study his riding. The fight lasted to the very end, when Daijiro passed Harada at the final corner on the final lap.

In the '01 season Daijiro won eleven out of sixteen races, to take the World Championship title 49 points ahead of his rival.

Team Gresini after winning the
250cc World Championship in 2001.
(Hidenobu Takeuchi)

Fausto Gresini

Manager of Team Gresini

Daijiro is always with me, in my heart

The first time I saw Daijiro was at the Japanese GP in 1996, when he entered the event as a wild-card rider, but it was winter 2000 when I first spoke to him. I went to pick him up at Bologna airport. He'd come to Italy for the team presentation. He looked worried and miserable then, like a lost child. Daijiro couldn't speak Italian and we couldn't speak Japanese, so we were worried at first, but it didn't matter at all. Daijiro was very good at gesturing.

In '01, when Daijiro was racing against Tetsuya Harada, we found out how strong Daijiro was mentally. We knew that he could win the World Championship, but we didn't expect him to win eleven races out of sixteen. The most memorable race that year was the Pan Pacific GP at Motegi. Daijiro was involved in a crash with Marco Melandri and his points advantage decreased a lot. But he won the next two GPs, in Australia and Malaysia, and won the championship.

After winning the championship, Daijiro sent me a letter which began 'My dear Italian father'. In it he said, 'Thank you very much for thinking not only of me but also of Maki and Ikko as your family. I am really grateful for the perfect environment which you prepared for me.' I was really impressed by that letter.

To win the MotoGP World Championship is hard work, so we had been preparing the structure needed for Daijiro to be successful. Daijiro was like my child, and it seems as though I watched him grow up from a child to an adult. Losing him was a shock which I cannot express in words. Daijiro is always with me, in my heart.

Fabrizio Cecchini

Mechanic with Team Gresini

I am feeling worse as time goes by

I saw Daijiro at the '96 Japanese GP. He was taking part in the 250cc race as a wild-card rider and I watched from the pit box with Alex Barros, who I was working for at that time. We were saying, 'Hey, look! He looks so young, young as a baby.' Daijiro finished third in the race and got on the podium. His hair was long and he looked so young but his eyes were sparkling and I could see he had something special about him.

Daijiro joined Team Gresini in 2000 and I became his chief mechanic in '01. At the beginning, he could not speak Italian so we had to communicate by gesture. But it worked out: Daijiro was very good at gesturing and I understood exactly what he wanted to say. However, his Italian improved and it was a great help for us to understand each other more.

Daijiro was such a talented rider and his 250cc races were all good. The happiest memory for me was the '01 Malaysian GP when he won the 250cc World Championship. But I was more impressed when he started to ride the NSR500. We expected him to take more time to get used to the 500cc machine, but he clocked a lap record at one of the off-season tests, although the tyres he was using were just standard ones. Daijiro was particular about engine settings. He was really fast when the engine settings were right. The bond between me and Daijiro was so strong and I loved him as I love my children. To me, his death will never be overcome. I am feeling worse as time goes by.

Immediately after the championship-winning race in Malaysia, 2001: Fausto Gresini was especially delighted. *(Hidenobu Takeuchi)*

ABOVE: Portuguese GP, 2001: chief mechanic Fabrizio Cecchini raises Daijiro aloft.
(Shigeo Kibiki, SKP Inc.)

OPPOSITE: Daijiro with Fausto Gresini at Sepang, 21 October 2001. *(Hidenobu Takeuchi)*

Hitoshi Tagawa

Mechanic with Team Gresini

Dai-chan was fast even in the rain

I began working in 250cc GP racing in 1993 with Tadayuki Okada and Tohru Ukawa. In 2000, Dai-chan was planning to go to GPs and I became chief mechanic for him.

In those days Dai-chan was expecting a machine like the one which he rode in the last race of the All Japan Championship in 1999. The feeling of that bike must have been perfect for him. But the new bike's suspension was completely different, the spec greatly changed, so at first we had to make him understand that we weren't able to make it the same. Basically he was consistently clear in what he demanded, so it was easy to know what he wanted. The point was, how would we cope with his problems.

The riders who aim for the top in GP racing are all strong individuals. We've known many difficult riders, but Dai-chan had a mild nature so I felt comfortable working with him.

The Brazilian GP is my best memory. We had selected the tyre to use for the race, but in the morning warm-up session we found our choice was no good, so we needed to decide on a tyre change in a hurry. But the tyre Dai-chan and I picked was different from the one suggested by other staff and the specialist from the tyre manufacturer. We had to make up our minds which tyre to select for our set-up. Finally, we made our choice for the race. I was stressed out about the decision, and the set-up we had, but Dai-chan just blew those feelings away and brought us victory.

Some people have said that Dai-chan was no good in wet conditions. I don't agree with them. He was never slow in any of our wet-weather tests. Actually, he was quite often the quickest. If he had a bike with a good set-up, he was a rider that could produce the best times in any conditions.

There was a time when I waited in the box for a long time to talk to him about changing the setting, but he didn't show up at all. He was taking a nap! So I had to go to his motorhome and wake him up to ask about the bike. I didn't think it was possible that he could sleep after riding that machine, for nerves.

When Dai-chan got off the machine, he was just like anyone else. Lots of people did not realise he was Daijiro Kato. One day, we went to a car-rental reception desk to pick up a car. Later the receptionist guy recognised Dai-chan from his signature on the form and was very surprised. Such cases happened quite often. He became popular after he debuted in GPs, but he was never a big head. That was his charm.

Incidentally, he was no good at driving a car. When we began to live in Europe, Daijiro drove a convertible Mercedes which Gresini had prepared for him – but soon he'd completely destroyed it. Mori (a mechanic) and I were shocked because we were both in the car: luckily we were all OK, but the car was completely crushed out of shape. The Italian polizia laughed and said, 'You are good on two wheels but not four.' It appeared as a big article in the Italian newspaper next morning. Later I was also told by one of the Honda staff, 'You must be careful!!'

Well, that year, Dai-chan was the rider for Team Gresini, a satellite team, but I wanted him to join a factory team. Factory teams and satellite teams are obviously not the same. When something happens, the speed of solution is entirely different between the teams. If he'd been with the factory team in 2000, I am sure he would have been able to win the title then – Dai-chan was a rider who had so much potential to be a winner – and then he would have been able to carry his career a stage further, up to 500cc straight away in 2001, if he had been 250cc champion in 2000. There is regret in my heart, that we were not able to make him a champion in his first year in GPs.

Australian GP, 2000: chief mechanic,
Hitoshi Tagawa, checks the condition
of Daijiro's bike. *(Shigeo Kibiki, SKP Inc.)*

The newly crowned 250cc World Champion. *(Shigeo Kibiki, SKP Inc.)*

Shinya Nakano

MotoGP racer

I wanted to be able to talk naturally to him someday

When I was seven or eight years old I went to Tsukuba circuit to watch a race where my friend was competing and met Daijiro there for the first time. My friend was his rival in the pocket bike class. Daijiro was already famous as a fast rider. I did not have a chance to run the same races while I was in the pocket bike class but I raced him in the mini bike class. In the All Japan Championship series 250cc class I raced a Yamaha, while he raced a Honda; we were rivals all the time.

His riding style was quite different from others even at that time. I used to watch him to see what was different and realised he was different, just after the exit of turns in particular. It was his excellent riding technique rather than his light weight that made him so different.

In 1998 I won the Japanese Championship but he was not going so well, and in 1999 I stepped up to the GPs first. In 2000 Daijiro and I raced in the 250cc GP class. Whenever I improved my time in qualifying he did so too. We were excellent rivals. I always kept my eye on him.

What I remember most is the Pacific GP race at Motegi in October 2000 when Daijiro took a win and I finished second. It was kind of a race where we fought to settle the long-term battle we'd started in the All Japan Championship. He was so good at acceleration that I was outdistanced by him at every exit of the turns. I was following his machine's tail closely, asking myself, 'Why? What is wrong with me?' I was really disappointed. I could only say 'hello' every time I saw him at the Grand Prix races. I thought I could not go any further as long as each of us represented different motorcycle manufacturers. But I wanted to be able to talk naturally to him someday, so I feel so sad. 'Can I hold my head up to Daijiro with my riding?' I am always wondering that to myself.

One of Kato's opponents in the 250cc World Championship in 2000 was Shinya Nakano. Here Daijiro is battling with him for the win at the Pacific GP; Nakano finished second. *(Shigeo Kibiki, SKP Inc.)*

Nakano could not catch Kato during the 2000 Pacific GP. *(Shigeo Kibiki, SKP Inc.)*

Daijiro won the Rio GP in 2000. The team welcomed him back to the pits: Michela Fabbri, the team's press manager, is wearing sunglasses; on her right, mechanic Ryoichi Mori. *(Shigeo Kibiki, SKP Inc.)*

French GP, 2001. Daijiro was the winner, with Harada second and Marco Melandri third. *(Shigeo Kibiki, SKP Inc.)*

Catalunya GP, 2001: Kato and Harada fought to the finish. *(Shigeo Kibiki, SKP Inc.)*

Harada was impressed by Daijiro's clever tactics at Catalunya in '01. *(Shigeo Kibiki, SKP Inc.)*

Marco Melandri

MotoGP racer

Daijiro and Tetsuya, they were the true champions

In 2001, when Daijiro and Tetsuya Harada were fighting for the 250cc World Championship, I joined battle with them many times and had lots of chances to watch their riding from behind.

Daijiro always rode his NSR250 as though he were glued to it. His riding style was very clean and perfect. He didn't look so fast, but in fact he was very fast. He didn't look aggressive even when he was battling with another rider. I guess he was better at winning on his own than dicing to the end with other guys. On the other hand, Tetsuya was always fast when his machine setting was right. Tetsuya was a true fighter but could not overcome difficulties when he had problems with his machine.

In Germany in '01 I won the race by beating Daijiro. I was also five seconds behind Daijiro in South Africa before the final lap and I caught up with him but couldn't beat him and he won the race. Those two races are the most memorable ones for me of the 2001 season.

I think Daijiro and Tetsuya were equal in their riding ability. Daijiro won more races than Tetsuya, but Daijiro had better equipment. Both Daijiro and Tetsuya were sincere, honest and kind people. I think they were the true champions.

Michela Fabbri

Team Gresini press officer

From the start I could understand what he was thinking

I first met Dai-chan at Bologna airport in February 2000. I went to pick him up with the team manager, Fausto Gresini. At the arrival area, he was trying to make a phone call using a public phone. He looked worried and his face was pale. I approached him and introduced myself. At that time, he couldn't speak much English and we couldn't speak Japanese. But I could understand what he was thinking by looking into his eyes. It was a strange feeling, though.

From then on, all the members of the team loved him and I started to teach him Italian. One day he said to me, 'Ciao, Mamma Michela', and I was so pleased. Yes, I was more or less a mother to him, rather than a team press officer.

The most memorable race for me was the Pacific GP in '00. Dai-chan crashed heavily during the timed practice on Saturday afternoon. His machine was badly damaged and the mechanics worked throughout the night to repair it. Next day, Dai-chan was battling against Shinya Nakano of Yamaha and won the race in the end.

Dai-chan never got nervous before the start of a race. He was always natural and cool. He knew exactly what he had to do. He was born to be a winner. He was so natural that some people said that he was like a robot or an alien. But instead, he was always warm and gentle. He made us happy all the time. And now, I really miss him. I am still crying. Dai-chan, I want to see you again…

AFRICA'S

Perhaps Harada is saying, 'Dai-chan, you were really fast!' They trusted each other completely.
(Shigeo Kibiki, SKP Inc.)

Tetsuya Harada

Ex-250cc World Champion

I looked forward to seeing him racing against Vale

I thought he had a riding style a bit similar to mine. Since then I've been very conscious of Daijiro, I guess. I have paid attention to him since he made his debut in the All Japan Championship. He was as fast as I expected; I would have signed him up first if I had organised my own Grand Prix team. He didn't have much opportunity to come to the GPs, but once there he put in excellent performances, as everyone had expected. He had an aura in the paddock that somehow made me feel I could not leave him alone, so I often used to talk to him.

In 2001, because of Aprilia's plans, I switched from 500cc to 250cc and finally met Daijiro in the same class. Winning the championship was my final goal. I thought I would be able to run wonderful races with him in the class. Among many other overseas riders who aggressively try to squeeze in or bump into you, Daijiro's beautiful and fair way of riding impressed me all the more. We had many good battles and every race is still vivid to me, but asked to pick one maybe it would be the race at Catalunya, where the two of us built a huge lead. I was going to overtake him at the final turn on the last lap but he outmanoeuvred me and completely bore me down. I never saw such a tactical rider. 'This guy looks innocent but actually he's pretty shrewd,' I thought. I was surprised that he kept calm enough to judge the situation. I fought Vale, Max Biaggi, Loris Capirossi and Daijiro for championship titles, and Daijiro was one of the most impressive riders. His riding style was so beautiful, and I particularly liked it.

I knew he was having a hard time in the 500cc class as I have a body shape like his and had the same trouble. As I am not as long limbed as Vale I cannot bring the machine under full control or lean it so easily. But I believed I could fully exert my potential once the machine had the right setting. Setting became much more important than in the 250s, and I had to stick to it more. Daijiro maybe needed more time and experience but the point was how the people around him were going to put everything in place for him rather than what he needed to do. I was sure he could match up to Vale once these conditions were met and I looked forward to the two racing against each other.

I retired in 2002 and was at home in Monaco in 2003 watching the opening round of the championship on TV. Just after the start of the race, when footage showed Daijiro lying down, I realised the situation was serious. 'What can it have been like, to make his boots come off? Why is the red flag not being waved for such a serious accident?' I called my friends in Japan but no one had details of the accident. As time went by I came to understand how seriously he was injured. I could not do anything but pray for his recovery.

While Daijiro was battling with injury I called somebody every day to ask about his condition. He must have fought very hard to survive for two weeks. I thought of his last weeks when I received the news of his death. I tried to get a ticket to return but, due to the Easter holiday, it was not until several days after the funeral services that I was able to visit his house and pray for him in front of his ashes and a picture of a smiling Daijiro. My name emerged as a possible fill-in for Daijiro and I was rumoured to have accepted the offer, but I'd never have thought of riding his machine. I hated somebody else riding my machine and I believe Daijiro would have felt the same way.

MotoGP 2002

NSR500/RC211V

In 2002, the blue ribbon class in the World Championship became the MotoGP class, for both four-stroke 990cc and two-stroke 500cc machines. Honda gave its four-stroke machine, the RC211V, to Valentino Rossi, the World Champion from the year before, and to Tohru Ukawa. However, the difference in potential between the RC211V and the NSR500 was noticeable even before the start of the season. Daijiro, riding the NSR500, struggled but still finished second behind Valentino Rossi on the RC211V in the Spanish GP at Jerez, the third round of the season.

At Brno, after the summer holiday break, Daijiro was also given an RC211V. He went to the Czech Republic after a brief position adjustment procedure at the Tochigi Honda test course. Daijiro was second in qualifying behind the master of Brno, Max Biaggi. With Daijiro so fast from the beginning, there were articles in Italian newspapers quoting Valentino Rossi as saying that Daijiro must have had a test somewhere and had to be lying about it being the first time he'd ridden the machine. Daijiro finished second in the race too, behind Biaggi.

During the post-race press conference Daijiro said he would win the next race, which led to applause from the audience of reporters from all over the world. Unfortunately for Daijiro, however, rainy races and machine trouble at the Pacific GP at Motegi meant there were no more wins for him that season. He would have to wait until 2003 for his first win on the RC211V…

Daijiro joined Team Gresini in 2000 and he grew up with the team In 2002, Daijiro moved up to the MotoGP class. *(Team Gresini)*

Mick Doohan

Ex-500cc World Champion

Daijiro had what it takes to become a World Champion

I first saw Daijiro during the Suzuka Eight Hour endurance race. I don't remember which year. I was at Suzuka doing promotional work for Honda. I remember a boy, who looked like a 13-year-old, was riding a Superbike machine incredibly fast. I kept my eye on him after that.

Daijiro's riding style was very smooth and it didn't look fast, but his lap times were really fast. He was the fastest rider during the year he won the 250cc World Championship. That was his image then, so when he moved up to the MotoGP class, everybody expected him to be as good as he was on a 250. That may have put some pressure on him. Daijiro was small so he could show his talent fully on a 250 machine but couldn't repeat it on MotoGP bikes. I think he had to try very hard to handle a big four-stroke machine. However, his riding style was very smooth and he was far better than the other Japanese riders, except Tady Okada. One thing I feel sorry about is he didn't like racing in the rain, for some reason.

I always say that the most important thing it takes to become a World Champion is to keep your determination. Daijiro had this and he showed it to the end. If he had won a race, he would have regained his confidence and won more. Maybe he could have won the championship, but the accident ended that possibility. Suzuka is not one of the safest tracks, but the place where Daijiro crashed is not the most dangerous spot there. If something had been different, he might have survived without any serious injury. I think the accident was a very unfortunate one.

Max Biaggi

MotoGP racer

Daijiro's riding style resembled mine

Daijiro was faster than anybody else, when he was riding 250cc.

His riding was smooth and many people have said his riding style resembled mine. During the Czech GP in '02, when Daijiro rode the RC211V for the first time, his lap times were faster than Rossi's and Rossi was shocked when he heard that. I was also surprised to see Daijiro's lap times.

I heard about Daijiro's accident after the race and I was destroyed. That night, I had a fan club party and there were almost fifty fans gathered for me. Instead of saying 'Cheers' for the opening of the party, I said:'Let's wish "Get well soon" to Daijiro.' I was worried about Daijiro that night and I waited until three or four o'clock in the morning for Dr Costa to come back to the hotel lobby. I couldn't sleep at all that night. Next morning, I had a talk with Nobuatsu Aoki and Kenny Roberts Jnr about having a safety meeting when we got to South Africa. Once the meeting got under away, I let the other riders control it.

While Daijiro was still in a coma, one Japanese fan came to me and gave me a Daijiro replica helmet. He said he wanted me to keep it. I have it in my office in Monaco, together with my own trophies. Daijiro was one of the nice people in the paddock. We don't see many nice people there nowadays. Daijiro was quite good at Italian, so I spoke with him quite often. Just before the Japanese GP, Daijiro and I were with Makoto Tamada and Makoto was surprised when Daijiro spoke to me in Italian. Makoto didn't understand Italian so he looked startled. It was so funny to see him then. I wish there were more nice people like Daijiro in the paddock.

Kato chases Valentino Rossi (46) during the 2002 Czech GP. Daijiro finished second on his first outing on the RC211V; Rossi retired with mechanical trouble. *(Shigeo Kibiki, SKP Inc.)*

OPPOSITE: Czech GP, 2002: Max Biaggi (3) won the race, with Daijiro finishing second.
(Shigeo Kibiki, SKP Inc.)

Teruaki Matsubara

HRC engineer

Rossi was always checking Dai-chan's lap times

I was in charge of development of the RC211V at HRC (Honda Racing Corporation) and I joined Valentino Rossi's team in 2002.

Rossi was always checking Dai-chan's lap times. In the first half of the season Rossi rode the RC211V while Dai-chan's bike was the NSR500. But still Rossi compared Dai-chan's time with his time of the year before: 'What spec is he using this time? My lap time was like this last year...' he kept saying.

At the Brno GP after the summer break, when Dai-chan received his RC211V for the first time, Rossi was anxious to confront Dai-chan. 'What is his lap time? Which tyre is he going to use?' Every time free and qualifying practice sessions finished, Rossi came to our box asking about Dai-chan. On Saturday, Dai-chan ended up second behind Max Biaggi in the qualifying session, but Rossi was quicker for the average lap time. I think he was nervous at that time, too. In the race, Rossi retired due to tyre delaminating problems, which had never happened before. Rossi knew that Dai-chan was chasing him from behind, so maybe he might have tried too hard, gone faster and made the pace too quick – and that's why his tyre became like that. I think that Rossi recognised Dai-chan's talent, because when Alex Barros started to ride the RC211V, from the Motegi GP (the Pacific GP), Rossi did not bother about Alex at all.

I have two good memories of Dai-chan's races. One is the 250cc race when Dai-chan beat Shinya Nakano. The other one was Dai-chan finishing second at Jerez: riding the NSR500 he caught up the group of four-strokes ahead of him in the race and clung on to them.

As an HRC engineer I developed machines thinking that Daijiro would be the next rider challenging Rossi. I wanted a Japanese rider to win the MotoGP title someday...

Kazuto Sakata

Ex-125cc World Champion

A rider of genius beyond imagination

When Daijiro made his debut in the All Japan Championship with Team Kotake I got a sort of intuition about him that reminded me of when I saw Tetsuya Harada racing for the first time. I was certain Daijiro would become fast. His way of riding was beautiful and smooth but once he had a chance to overtake he got the job done. He did not say much and was quiet, but on the other hand he never got stage fright no matter how big an event he was running in. I think he was aggressive enough to maximise his potential in races.

In terms of his sense of riding he was just a genius beyond imagination. When I switched from Honda to Aprilia I was confused at the larger size, even though both of these machines have the same 125cc displacement. But every time he stepped up he soon learned to manipulate a bigger machine. I understand why Valentino Rossi is fast. It can easily be imagined that his arms and legs allow him to control a machine in a case like this, and recover if the machine gets out of control, but as to how Daijiro handled those big machines with his stature I cannot imagine. I know how difficult it is for a rider of small stature to balance himself on a big machine. I couldn't see myself running like Daijiro on a 500cc or a MotoGP racer. He must have managed by weight-shifting to keep the machine under control in a way that no one could imagine. The more I realise how outstanding he was the more I get to feel overwhelmed. I believe Daijiro would have been a World Champion in the top motorcycle class.

Daijiro leaves the pits on the RC211V at the '02 Czech GP. *(Shigeo Kibiki, SKP Inc.)*

Daijiro rode the RC211V for the first time at the '02 Czech GP. He was so fast that many people didn't believe it was his first outing on the machine. *(Team Gresini)*

Noboru Ueda

Ex-125cc GP racer

Dai-chan brought peace to the paddock

I met Dai-chan for the first time when he was just a high school boy. I had already heard about him, and that he was fast, so when I first met him I walked up to him and said, 'Go for it!

We had a connection because we were contracted to the same helmet company (Shoei), and we often attended the same events for advertising activities. When we went to Kyushu together, we took a picture sticker (at a picture booth called the Print Club), selecting a monkey costume to dress up in. It was a good memory anyway. Dai-chan had a taciturn image, but actually he was a guy who also had a witty, hilarious side.

When I saw his smile in the paddock I was so relieved for some reason. He was loved by everyone: Dai-chan was the kind of man who brought peace to the paddock.

One day I had a good time playing games with Haruchika (Aoki) and Dai-chan and their wives. Dai-chan was a cool guy, but whenever he played TV games, he struggled hard. He was so funny and we could not stop laughing at him, you know. You must drink if you are defeated in a game, it was a kind of penalty, and Dai-chan got completely drunk. It was fun.

I think that he was a fair rider and he rode very cleanly, never blocking another rider's line. That is one impression of him. I think that his pursuit of riding was at a very high level.

In addition, I expected him to come to GP racing earlier. He should have. Surely lots of offers must have been made to him. He came to GPs after a long wait, and became 250cc World Champion, and finally started in the highest class. He wanted his dream to come true. He was a rider who had a future, a truly wonderful future … I cannot say anything … no words…

Youichi Ui

Grand Prix racer

He was like my younger brother

I am an only child and Daijiro was the same, so he was like my younger brother.

I came to know him when he was riding a mini bike but it was not until he came to Grand Prix racing that we became close. It was me who wired up the TV set of his motorhome for him. He looked very happy when the TV worked successfully. We were almost always together during away tours, driving a rent-a-car, going out to borrow a cell phone, or eating out. He was amazing in racing, but in his personal life he did nothing, I mean it's like he would rather say, 'Yes, please' if someone was going to do something for him. But I didn't mind looking after him. I even enjoyed the away tours!

I became a father first. Daijiro saw me playing with Yohei and said, 'I want kids.' 'If you want, you'll soon have them,' I answered. At the end of the year Ikko was born. I think he was a good daddy as he played a lot with Ikko and called his family very often when he was away from them. He loved his family.

One day at Suzuka I asked him, 'How is the new chicane?' 'Hmm...' – he was lost for words. 'OK, OK, I was wrong. I shouldn't have asked you.' And we both laughed. I can't believe he is no longer here. I believed he would get better. I wanted to take him on someday. He manipulated big machines so easily with his small stature. That inspired me to set high goals. On a tour in 2003, after his accident, it was so painful to remember him that I stayed at completely different hotels than usual. But now I carry Daijiro's picture. It's hard both to remember and to forget him.

Daijiro Kato

Everybody expected Daijiro to win on the RC211V sooner or later — but it never happened. *(Team Gresini)*

Akira Ryo

Suzuki works rider

I think Daijiro was born to race

I became aware of Daijiro at the second round of the 1994 All Japan Championship at Mine. My maiden Superbike win obviously makes the event special for me, but his riding in 250cc race makes it memorable as well. He took pole and led the field until he fell down on the final lap.

Many of my generation earned their living and saved money to race, but Daijiro was different. Ever since he could remember, a motorcycle had been his plaything and there had been races all the time. He spent his whole childhood racing and then came to run in the Grands Prix. He was living in the paddock with his family. He only knew racing and there was only racing for him. Racing was his life. I think Daijiro was born to race.

In 2002 I was also running in GPs. Daijiro adapted himself to the Grand Prix paddock. He spoke Italian, Spanish and English very well. I was surprised to find him managing to communicate with everyone. I didn't think he had such vitality, to survive in foreign countries. I only ran in several GP races and didn't find myself comfortable there, so he looked all the more brilliant.

I was at Suzuka when the accident happened. My eyes were glued to the monitor. I was feeling the urge to rescue him. One second seemed like ages. 'Why is the red flag not being waved?' It was on about lap 6 when an ambulance arrived, and it was only on the fifth or sixth lap before the end of the race that the helicopter took off with him on board. I can clearly remember being so impatient with the rescue effort. I still wonder why such an accident happened and how it could have been avoided. We have to address the issues Daijiro's accident raised and find answers.

Hikaru Miyagi

Ex-HRC racer

Daijiro had the best riding style of our time

If I'd achieved great success like Daijiro I would have been more outgoing at press conferences. But he didn't say much. He seemed to have cooled right down by the time he got to the podium after taking the chequered flag. I always wondered how big the gap was between his excellent riding and his relaxed manner in normal life. But from late 2002 he had significantly increased his presence as a rider and his sense of responsibility as a man. I was really looking forward to his future career.

The essence of his riding lay in its beauty. I could find nothing wrong with his riding from reading magazines and newspapers, or even watching him on TV. It was perfectly beautiful from any angle. His head and body were positioned perfectly for the bike. He maximised the machine's power with minimal handling – well balanced and no needless movement. He figured out instantly how to get maximum performance from the motorcycle and put it into practice, so he appeared to ride easily. Top athletes and racers appear to move easily so people assume they can as well, but in fact it is quite difficult. Daijiro was one of those top sporting figures. He must have been the ideal rider for engineers as well, because he stuck closely with the machine to get the best out of it. He never twisted or wriggled around. He had the riding style that engineers wanted their racers to have.

I think Daijiro's riding was as excellent as that of Kenny Roberts, the man whom every rider once longed to be – the best riding style of our time. It is a feeling I don't get from Valentino Rossi or Max Biaggi, something that I can feel only from Daijiro.

Kato on a two-stroke NSR500 was faster than Tohru Ukawa on a four-stroke RC211V during the '02 Spanish Moto GP race at Jerez. *(Team Gresini)*

The Fortuna team's hospitality tent. Daijiro can be seen bottom right. *(Team Gresini)*

OPPOSITE TOP: In the pits during free practice. *(Team Gresini)*

OPPOSITE BOTTOM: Daijiro leading Ukawa (11) at the Spanish GP in 2002. *(Shigeo Kibiki, SKP Inc.)*

Daijiro retired from the Pacific GP in
'02 with mechanical trouble.
(Shigeo Kibiki, SKP Inc.)

Kenny Roberts Snr

Ex-500cc World Champion

We also wanted Daijiro on our team

I had few chances to talk to Daijiro but I could see that he was a talented rider, by watching him racing. He was one of those rare riders who can control his speed. In other words, he could control races. Not only could he ride fast, but he could also ride slower and cleaner. This is a rare ability which only a few riders, such as Valentino Rossi, Max Biaggi and Kenny Roberts Jnr, have at the moment in the MotoGP class.

Like other teams, we at ProtonKR also wanted Daijiro. We were thinking of approaching him at the end of 2002, but we gave up the idea because our team structure was not good enough then to invite him. Honda would not have let us take him away.

I believe Daijiro could have won the MotoGP championship. His chances were ruined by that accident at Suzuka and I feel sorry about it. Daijiro should have come to the World Championships earlier. Honda should have brought him sooner.

There will be more Japanese riders to follow Daijiro. They should have more experience of dirt track and off-road riding. The situation in Japan is still almost twenty years behind the situation in the USA.

Kenny Roberts Snr was someone else who was impressed by Kato's riding skill. *(Team Gresini)*

1976–1993
From Akigase to the Kyushu Championship

It was very hot on 4 July 1976, the day Daijiro was born. He was the first child of Takashi and Hatsumi Kato. In fact, he was their only child and they loved him deeply. They were eager to teach him many kinds of sport. Daijiro started learning to swim when he was just nine months old. At three, he started learning a Japanese martial art known as budo. Although his parents did not know anything about racing, they gave Daijiro a pocket bike as a present for his third birthday. This present marked the start of Daijiro's career. His cousin, Chojun Kameya, also began to ride pocket bikes. They started racing together at the age of four at Akigase circuit, in their local Saitama area.

They had a lot of friends at Akigase circuit, which is owned by the Motoyama family, including the Motoyama brothers, Satoshi and Tomomi, and the Takeda brothers, Makoto and Yuichi. At that time, pocket bike racing was very popular in Japan. Races were held all over the country, and there were usually more than a hundred entries for each race. Daijiro went on to become the national pocket bike champion. Then, at the age of 11, he moved up to mini bike racing, about the same time that Norick Abe became part of the Akigase racing scene.

In 1993, Daijiro graduated to road racing. He met Fukumi Kotake, a mentor and team owner who had already discovered many talented riders, including Akira Yanagawa and Tohru Ukawa. Daijiro joined Team Kotake in Kyushu, in the south-western part of Japan and a long way from Saitama. From Monday to Friday Daijiro went to high school in Saitama. Then he flew to Kyushu on Friday night after school. Although he didn't have much time to practise, he won all the races he took part in and was the victor in three classes in the championships. Daijiro also set lap records at many tracks in the Kanto Championship and the Suzuka Championship.

Daijiro became famous during 1993 and was top of the list for the '93 Suzuka Four Hour endurance race. Unfortunately, the race was wet and Daijiro went off the track. He did not win but, as a result of his splendid riding in the race, his reputation continued to grow.

Daijiro on a pocket bike.
(Takashi Kato)

Tomomi Motoyama

Daijiro's pocket bike coach

I never thought Daijiro himself liked motorcycles

As my parents ran Akigase circuit Satoshi, my younger brother, and I were always at the track. When I was a junior high school student Daijiro, at the age of four or five, came to the track. His father asked me to show him how to ride a motorcycle. Of course he was no good at riding at the beginning, but somehow he looked good. I told him to do 100 sit-ups for training – he easily accomplished that and could have done 200 or even more. It wasn't at all difficult for him. I always let him try a motorcycle before his father thought Daijiro was ready for it. I still remember he rode them as if he was hanging from them. His mother sometimes came along as we were about to close the circuit, saying, 'Sorry, but please let him ride just for five minutes!' As she said, his father would be angry if he did not ride every day. I laughed and said, 'You should come either five minutes earlier or five minutes later', but I kept them company.

In 2003, because of the Daijiro Cup, we had more opportunity to see old friends and felt like we'd returned to the old days. Daijiro's parents were enthusiastic but I never thought Daijiro himself liked motorcycles. So when I saw him training with a dirt bike at the beginning of 2003 I was surprised, but also impressed at how deeply he was committing himself to MotoGP. Suzuka is far away and we don't usually like going, but there was something that made all of us go there. We went along to cheer him.

I thought he wouldn't make it in the Japanese championships, no matter how fast he was at Akigase. And then I thought he wouldn't make it worldwide, no matter how fast he was in Japan. But, against all my expectations, he got faster and faster. I found myself becoming a fan of Daijiro's, and although I was a little embarrassed I kept cheering for him. In fact, I began to look forward to the day when he would become a World Champion.

Makoto Takeda

A pocket bike and mini bike friend

Daijiro remained Daijiro

My younger brother Yuichi and I started pocket bike racing at Akigase and we raced with Daijiro and some other riders. He was so smart, going for wins with the help of a good engine, or watching out for a last-minute chance to head home. In retrospect his racing was more like that of an adult than a child. As far as I remember he was never defeated, which means he was really fast!

Daijiro was the boss of the naughty kids, while my brother Yuichi, a year younger than Daijiro, was the errand boy and Jun (Kameya), who was the same age as Daijiro, was often made to cry by him. In most cases it was Daijiro who came up with the mischief. We were always scolded for it, but really I have only pleasant memories of having a lot of fun. It felt like being on a school trip while we were on away tours.

After quitting racing I came along to cheer for him. When Daijiro was defeated I just couldn't accept it and got annoyed. He was our hero. He liked being with friends, so whenever we had time we went to support him. When the Daijiro Cup started in 2003 we all got together again, as we felt that 'if we don't help him who is going to?'

He was a rider of genius but the best thing was probably that he had not changed at all since I first got to know him. Daijiro remained Daijiro, even though he became a World Champion and famous. He never acted big. He was kind, nice and considerate all his life.

Daijiro finished last at his first pocket bike race, but soon became more successful. *(Takashi Kato)*

OPPOSITE: Daijiro's pocket bike was often prepared at home: racing meant everything to his family.
(Takashi Kato)

Kazunori Bito

Owner of BRD

Daijiro passed Haruchika, and then went into the pits

Daijiro was in the fourth grade or so when I met him for the first time. He fell and hit his head in a mini bike race held in Gifu Prefecture. I got ice cubes from a woman I knew, who happened to prepare cold noodles, and put them on his head. Mini bike races were popular at that time, with Norick (Norifumi Abe), Yuichi Takeda, Tetsuya Harada, the three Aoki brothers as well as Daijiro fighting tough battles at the different tracks in Japan. The Aoki brothers, based in Gumma Prefecture, were some of the strongest rivals of my tuning shop. They were supremely fast and always bore away the winning prize of 30,000 yen.

Mitsuo Abe, Norick's father, bought his son an S50 from my shop in August 1989, and then Daijiro's father bought one for him in November – he'd had a ride on it and wanted one. He was getting faster and faster from that time. He and his friends always rode at Akigase until it got dark. They were playing around rather than practising, and looked really happy.

I looked after him for three years before he stepped up to the novice class. His father said from the beginning he would make his son a factory rider, preferably of the team owned by Erv Kanemoto. That's why he left his son in my hands, as a stepping stone towards that goal, I guess.

Daijiro's father's next plan was to send him to Team Kotake in Kyushu when he got into high school. We went to the HSR circuit to get the team to test him. His father and I took turns to drive the van. Of course Daijiro enjoyed a sound sleep in the back seat almost all the way! He was given an opportunity there to run a 90-minute endurance race for mini bikes with an NS50M. When he was allowed a special practice at the track on the day before the race we heard the course record was 2m 24s, but he set a best time of 2m 26s. In the race, however, the other riders only did 2m 34–35s, and he took a superb victory with a big lead of one lap after just the first few laps. The 'record' he was trying very hard to break turned out to be wrong! The displacement of his machine was alleged illegal, as he was too fast, and the engine had to be stripped. When it was proved to conform to the regulations everyone looked at him in a new light.

After he was accepted into Team Kotake there was the final round of a local championship at Mase, in which Daijiro and Haruchika Aoki both ran in the 125cc class on the RS125. It was Haruchika, the 'master' of Mase, who took pole, while Daijiro started from second on the grid. As he said to me, he just wanted not to lose out to Haruchika, so I made my very best efforts to tune up the engine. But he was not allowed to win the race by the team, as that would promote him to a higher class: he was set to run the Suzuka Four Hour endurance race in the following year as a novice rider with Team Kotake. Haruchika was faster in the straights but Daijiro was confident he would overtake him in the final turn, and he fulfilled his prediction by passing Haruchika in the final turn and then went into the pits on the following lap, keeping his place. That is a heroic episode, isn't it?

All mini bike folk at that time were inspired by Kevin Schwantz and copied his style of riding, but I stopped Daijiro doing that and told him it was Kenny Roberts's way of riding that he should learn from. Kenny is small as well, but manipulated machines so beautifully. I hoped Daijiro would ride that way. I still cannot look at his pictures. I am the same age as his father, so he was like my son.

Yes, I can still see the boys riding at Akigase until it got dark.

Daijiro with friends from Akigase circuit, including Norick Abe (*right*). (*Takashi Kato*)

OPPOSITE TOP: The top of the podium seemed to be reserved for Daijiro. (*Takashi Kato*)

OPPOSITE BOTTOM: Daijiro with Kazunori Bito, his mentor during the mini bike era. The rider on the left is Tsuyoshi Chiwa, Daijiro's friend. (*Naoyoshi Mizukawa*)

Tokuo Iobe

Owner of I-Factory

He already showed a glimpse of genius as a rider

I used to run a service shop for track meetings of the HRC club and consequently came along to provide physical training and organise some meetings at Sportsland-Sugo in the summer and at Suzuka in the off season. One summer Daijiro came to Sugo accompanied by Bito-san (Kazunori Bito) in an attempt to step up from mini bikes to road racing. He looked so little and cute that his entry was not accepted because the reception lady thought he was not old enough to take part. Bito-san said, 'He is fast', but I couldn't believe it at first. His racing activities were mainly in the Kyushu Championship and I was asked to look after him when he raced in the Kanto area, although it was only for one year that we went to the track together.

What Bito-san said was true. In the opening round at Tsukuba, Daijiro took a double win in the 125cc and 250cc classes. In one race he was leading the field but ended up crashing at the final corner on the last lap. He either took wins or crashed, but he was always fast throughout these series. On weekdays I used to warm up the pistons and the crankshaft so that he could ride on the machine as soon as he arrived at the track after school. His way of riding was smooth and consistent, and so I did not notice how fast he was until I looked at a stopwatch. I felt like I learned from Daijiro what riding a motorcycle meant.

His feedback was precise and to the point. It was not always easy to understand, but his judgement of the situation was exact. He was able to tell us what was happening to the machine, which helped mechanics to set the bike up quickly. We did not teach him anything or give advice to him. Undoubtedly he already showed a glimpse of genius as a rider.

Mitsuo Abe

Norifumi Abe's father and a Japanese speedway racer

He showed a natural riding ability from childhood

From my long experience in the motorcycle business I felt Daijiro's riding was perfect. He showed a natural ability from childhood, when I first met him, at a time when I was successful. I also remember he was always sleeping, apart from when he was riding a motorcycle.

When I took Nori (Norifumi) to Akigase, Daijiro's father spoke to me and that began our close family association. He looked after Nori when I could not travel with him because of my own races. When the kids were talking about sleeping over at Daijiro's place Nori was unwilling to join in at first, as he had never done so before. However, Daijiro, Jun (Kameya), Yuichi (Takeda) and Makoto, Yuichi's elder brother, encouraged him to try. After that everyone got together to race, like a training camp. Daijiro was really fast and everyone was inspired by him to go faster themselves. They used to practise at Akigase until it got dark, even when there were no races happening. They brushed up their skills by riding mini races or going anti-clockwise round the track. The kids were all good friends and seemed very happy together.

He called me 'Abe no ojichan' (a casual but friendly way of saying 'Mr Abe') until quite recently. From my standpoint as a senior rider I really wanted him to go to Grands Prix much earlier, to make the best use of his talents. If this had happened he would surely have had a totally different racing life. At Suzuka, when I asked him about his new-born daughter, he said 'I'm thinking of naming her Rinka and I'm going to register her birth after the race', and he showed me her picture. She looked just like Daijiro. Those turned out to be his last words to me.

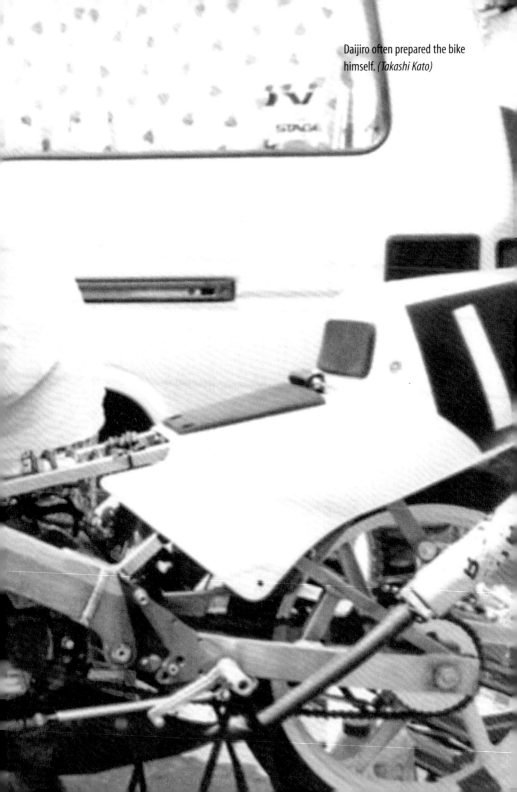

Daijiro often prepared the bike himself. *(Takashi Kato)*

Fukumi Kotake

Manager of Team Kotake

A dream of making history with victory in three classes

Kazunori Bito introduced a high school boy called Daijiro to me.

I enjoyed watching him as he started to produce very good lap times in succession. He was really fast. When I watched him riding I realised that he was a clever guy, although he didn't reply clearly when I asked him a question. Then I thought that he was a man who could make history.

We decided to participate in the All Kyushu Championship, aiming to win in three classes (racer 125, 250, production 250). Racing in three classes is really hard on a rider, both mentally and physically, but Daijiro's ability to ride smoothly and efficiently convinced me that he could do it.

The riders who join Team Kotake normally move to Kumamoto to live but Daijiro came over every weekend from Saitama, where his parents' home was. Travelling back and forth by plane must have been tough for him. However, Daijiro easily overcame such difficulties and he accomplished that victory in three classes. Then he stepped up to the All Japan Championship with Team Kotake, but I hoped he could join a factory team and go to the Grands Prix as soon as possible. I really wanted to let him go, because I honestly wanted him to become a World Champion. After Daijiro passed away I went to Italy with his father. I had a reason for going there: I needed to have a meeting with Fausto Gresini because my rider, Ryuichi Kiyonari, had been picked as Daijiro's replacement in the team. In Italy I experienced the special atmosphere created by Daijiro's fans and I saw how popular he was. I was also surprised to see that Via Daijiro (the street dedicated to him) was really beautiful and worthy of his name, even though it was still under construction. He was loved so much in Italy and everyone took good care of him. I think that the flame of the spirit of motorsport that was ignited by Daijiro should be nurtured and carried on.

Fukumi Kotake, owner of Team Kotake (*right*). Daijiro, Makoto Tamada and Ryuichi Kiyonari were all team graduates. *(Daijiro.net)*

Daijiro made a vow for the New Year: 'My dream is to become a motorcycle racer'. *(Takashi Kato)*

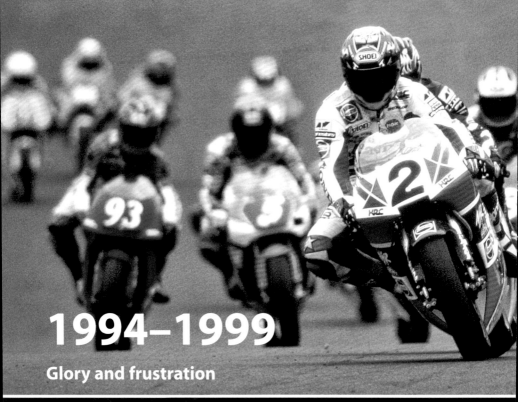

1994–1999

Glory and frustration

In 1994 Daijiro started taking part in the 250cc class of the All Japan Championship. He was riding a production racer Honda RS250, in a class where Honda, Yamaha and Suzuki factory machines were taking part. Daijiro took pole position in the opening round of the championship and he was leading the race until the last lap, when he crashed. Although he won his first race in the championship that year, at the TI Aida circuit, he crashed in 60 per cent of the races and finished seventh in the final points standings.

In '95 Daijiro moved up to a '94 model factory NSR250. He took pole position four times and won two races, finishing fifth in the final table. In '96 he achieved five pole positions and won four races, finishing second in the championship. He also finished third in the Japanese GP, in which he took part as a wild-card rider.

In 1997 Daijiro became an HRC factory rider. Unfortunately, he was in a car accident before the opening round of the All Japan Championship and was not able to race, but he returned for the Japanese GP and won the race, beating Tohru Ukawa and Tetsuya Harada. That year, he took pole position seven times in the All Japan Championship, was victorious in eight races and won the title.

All Japan Championship days.
(*Takashi Akamatsu*)

Many fans wanted Daijiro to move up to GPs in 1998, but Honda was keen for him to win the home title in consecutive years. The '98 NSR250 had a pivotless frame and was not easy to set up well. Despite that, however, Daijiro won the Japanese GP on it, again as a wild-card rider. He was the only rider in the world to win a race on that machine in 1998, but he sustained minor injuries during the season and could only finish eighth in the final All Japan Championship standings.

In '99, Daijiro fought the All Japan Championship against Naoki Matsudo, riding a Yamaha. Each ended up with the same number of wins and second places. Under the regulations in effect at the time the championship was decided by their final standings the previous year, when Naoki was third and Daijiro was eighth, so Matsudo won the title. The regulations were later changed, so that in a case where two riders were tied based on wins and second places, the championship would be decided by their positions in the final round. If the amended rule had been in effect in 1999, Daijiro would have become the champion, because he won the last round at Motegi with a huge margin over Matsudo.

Shinichi Ito

Ex-Grand Prix racer

One of his secrets was his remarkable physical ability

I met Daijiro for the first time at a Honda party. He was still a child, with a crew cut. When I saw him at an HRC training camp several years later I thought he was sharp in his movements, in other words he had brilliant reflexes. His riding style was already perfect when he moved up to the All Japan Championship. His set-up was unique as well. His way of riding particularly caught my eye, as he rode a 250 as though he were riding a 500. He was able to come out of corners in the shortest time by instantly setting the motorcycle upright to accelerate out of the corner. It was his remarkable physical ability that allowed him to ride that way. His body moved quickly in response to every change of situation. Tetsuya Harada was fast because he was smart, while Daijiro was fast because of his quick reflexes. His concentration while riding was amazing, although he was always sleeping and often started riding with sleepy eyes. I used to wonder when he switched to racing mode.

When we went to Malaysia together for a test Daijiro drew some pictures of Ampanman (a popular cartoon character) very well on a disposable tablecloth he found at breakfast. I was surprised at this unexpected skill. When he visited my car shop in Sendai, he crashed into a truck as he tried to change lanes, and his car was written off. It was a serious accident but he came away smiling, without a scratch, and really proved he was something special. I would never sit next to him when he was driving a car, though!

In racing he was faster on the straights than me, because he was lighter. After he passed me on the straight during an Eight Hour endurance race, he turned around and said sorry to me. He was lovable as a person. In my long career in racing I never heard anyone speak badly of him. I guess nobody can be liked or loved by everyone as he was.

Yukio Kagayama

British and World Superbike Championship racer

Daijiro was full of wonders

I have a memory of being completely beaten by Daijiro in a mini bike race. I could hardly stand being defeated by such a youngster! However, I was much better at mountain biking, which we started together after we had both grown up. In fact he didn't stand out much except for motorcycles, I guess, and that was what made him so cute.

I've studied motorcycles very hard since I realised I was not a genius at riding, and so I wanted to find out what Daijiro's secrets were, because he was a rider of genius. He was full of wonders. It was in his motorhome in the middle of the Valencia test during the off season in 2003 that I finally sat and talked to him. He said as little as before, but he spoke in earnest and I was surprised to find he had a good understanding of mechanical things. He said although we tend to stick to settings to build up a faster motorcycle, making the best use of the existing one would facilitate the set-up, that is, he would rather help the machine progress by changing his own approach. At that moment I felt I was in touch with some of his secrets. And then I largely changed my view of him, finding out that this rider of genius was thoughtful and making efforts.

My first victory in the All Japan Championship was in the 1997 opening session, which Daijiro missed as he was in hospital after a car accident. Of course I was glad to win, but I wondered who would give me credit for winning the race without him. I will always regret that I've missed my chance to realise my ambition of racing with him and taking a win. I could not stop crying on the day when I heard he had passed away. Later, I also had a serious crash and was hovering between life and death. Thankful for still being alive, I have to keep making an effort to come closer to his pace in order to fulfil my responsibility for knowing his secrets.

In 1995 Daijiro competed successfully
as a privateer and took two wins.
(Takashi Akamatsu)

Daijiro started to take part in the All Japan Championship in 1994. *(Takashi Akamatsu)*

In '95 Kato was riding the NSR250. *(Takashi Akamatsu)*

Noriyasu Numata

Ex-All Japan 250cc Champion

Daijiro helped me to maintain focus

When I heard about a novice rider doing 59–60s laps at Tsukuba I could hardly believe it. Daijiro was a wonder rider. Actually, he was still a cute little boy in high school. I tried to talk to him but all he would say was 'Hmm...' or 'Haw'. I wondered, 'Is he really fast?'

However, I was amazed at his good sense and the reliable technique he displayed in the All Japan Championship. The advent of such a gifted rookie made me feel tense. I just couldn't lose out to a junior riding a production racer, even though it was a kit bike. Daijiro helped me to maintain focus. His presence allowed me to improve. Having great fights with Kyoji Namba, Kensuke Haga, Tohru Ukawa, Chojun Kameya and Daijiro Kato is a good memory for me. Daijiro often fell down in his first All Japan Championship season, but he already had good pace and an innate racing sense that convinced me he would certainly become a world-class rider.

After I retired I became a fan of Daijiro's and kept cheering him in front of the TV, saying, 'You can do it. You hang in there to become a MotoGP champion!' I was glad when he moved up to the 500cc class, and in 2003 I really expected him to challenge for the podium or even the championship title, given his times. He would be the last rider to make an error. 'What exactly happened?' This question has bothered me ever since then. A lot of people attended the farewell ceremony and that made me realise again that Daijiro was a great guy. He was loved by everybody. I cannot forget him and wouldn't want to do that.

In '96 Daijiro won from pole position
in round 7, at the TI circuit. *(Takashi
Akamatsu)*

OPPOSITE: Daijiro won round 3, at
Tsukuba, from pole position in
(Takashi Akamatsu)

Takahiro Sohwa

Ex-All Japan Championship racer

He will be remembered as the best rider of our era

I started to ride motorcycles as a street rider and then started racing, while Daijiro had a racing bike available from childhood. It was natural for him to live a racing life that was not of his own choice, so he had no conception of riding street bikes or playing with motorcycles. When I tried to suggest doing those kind of things he was not very enthusiastic, or rather he had the idea of doing different things. I doubted he liked racing, and even thought he might hate motorcycles.

In mid-1999, however, he said, 'Now I can find pleasure in riding. Racing is getting more interesting for me as well.' Before that, of course, he must have been happy when he won and disappointed when he lost, but I felt after 1999 he was committed to racing. I was happy for him to be able to think that way, especially considering his previous successful achievements. I think he was truly a rider of genius. He did well in every big event, whenever I expected him to do so. Winning a Grand Prix race as a wild-card rider was never easy, no matter how familiar he was with the Suzuka circuit. The more we expected of him, the more he displayed his ability. He had the essential requirements of a hero. I am sure he will be remembered as the best rider of our era.

He also expressed great sympathy towards me. I don't know how many times a simple word from him gave me help and encouragement to give things another try. During tests for the Suzuka Eight Hour endurance race I was riding just behind him, and I was overwhelmed by his tremendous speed from the 130R to the chicane. I can still hardly believe that was where the accident happened. Although the track had just been revised it was the turn that he was best at. What really happened there? I want somebody to tell me.

By 1999 Daijiro was ready to step up to the Grands Prix. *(Takashi Akamatsu)*

Daijiro enjoyed mountain biking with Yukio Kagayama and Takahiro Sohwa. *(Daijiro.net)*

Kato was one of the top riders in the class in 1994. *(Takashi Akamatsu)*

In '96, in round 5 at Fuji Speedway, Daijiro was sixth in qualifying and won the race. *(Takashi Akamatsu)*

In round 2 in '94 at Mine Daijiro started from pole and led the race until the final lap, then crashed. *(Takashi Akamatsu)*

Naoki Matsudo

250cc Grand Prix racer

Daijiro was virtually the 1999 All Japan 250cc Champion

In the 1999 All Japan 250cc Championship Daijiro and I fought for the title as Honda and a Yamaha factory riders respectively. That was my best season, as at last I was able to ride a factory machine after my long career racing as a privateer. I was winning in the first half of the season, but in the latter part Daijiro did better. In the final round, at Motegi, we fought for the title. He was very fast, with as much as a two-second advantage over me in qualifying. He won the race and I finished second. Our points scores were even and we had the same number of wins and second places, so the previous year's ranking was taken into account and I became the champion. But, to be honest, I was not happy at all. It's true that I was the champion according to the regulations, but people who saw the two of us racing during the final round thought he deserved the honour. I must admit Daijiro was virtually the champion in 1999.

I was determined to compete against him in Grand Prix races. In 2000 both of us got GP seats but what I was given was a production machine, while Daijiro's motorcycle was a factory bike, so our races were not as close as those we'd had in the All Japan Championship. I still feel sorry that I couldn't show my full potential then. It was difficult to understand that he had gone ahead of me, even though we'd once raced on equal terms, but I believed I would have a chance to compete with him again as long as I kept racing. That will never happen now...

It is difficult for me to get close to other manufacturers' riders, but Daijiro was an exception. He was natural, kind to everyone and loved his family. At all times Daijiro remained Daijiro, and he had a good nature. He was my favourite rider.

Daijiro battled in the 1999 All Japan Championship against Naoki Matsudo (Yamaha). *(Takashi Akamatsu)*

Matsudo won the '99 championship. Here Daijiro celebrates with him on the podium. *(Takashi Akamatsu)*

In 1997 Daijiro took part in the Japanese GP as a wild card and won the 250cc race, beating Ukawa and Harada. *(Takashi Akamatsu)*

Toshiyuki Yamaji

HRC engineer

The day when Daijiro cried for the first time

I was chief mechanic to Daijiro in 1997 and 1998, when he was taking part in the All Japan 250cc Championship riding the NSR250; 1997 was his first year as an HRC factory rider and he won eight races out of ten. He missed the opening round, though, because he was involved in a car accident the day before the race and suffered a serious injury to his head that required several stitches.

The next race scheduled for him was the Japanese GP and he was to take part in that as a wild-card rider, like the previous year. He went to Suzuka circuit straight from a hospital in Suzuka city. Whether he would participate in the race or not depended on his condition. His riding was stable, even though he was taking a painkilling injection. He qualified third and the team staff were saying, 'If we're lucky, we can score a podium finish.' But then he won the race! Daijiro was third on the penultimate lap, then he came out ahead of the front runners quite smoothly on the last lap, and won the race. 'Huh? Did he win?' I could hardly believe it. It was not until I found an article with a colour picture in the newspaper *Yomiuri Shinbun* on the following day that I really felt he'd done it.

After winning the Japanese GP, he won four consecutive races in the All Japan, but his streak ended in the next two races that were held in the wet. After that he won another four consecutive races and won the championship. We became more confident about his wins as the season approached its end. What we were cautious about was crashes, but he didn't crash so much that year.

At first I had a great deal of trouble understanding what Daijiro was trying to say. He didn't tell us what he wanted us to do for the suspension or which tyres to choose. His comments were unique rather than precise. They were things like 'the machine is like jelly' – to figure out what 'being like jelly' meant was just like solving a riddle. I gradually got used to Daijiro's phrases and came to know his way of finding the best settings.

We had a tough time in 1998 when the factory NSR250 was modified. Daijiro won the Japanese GP again, and maybe his win ironically slowed down the machine's development. Out of all his races in 1998, in the All Japan and the Grands Prix, Daijiro's win at the Japanese GP was his only victory that year. The most memorable race in 1998 for me was round 5 at Mine, the track which he was good at. He must have felt he couldn't win at the other tracks unless he won there. In the race he was trying too hard and crashed at the last turn on lap 1. I just couldn't talk to him when he came back to the pit crying. He looked so disappointed. Later on, he said it was very tough to keep up with Shinya Nakano, and admitted the crash was entirely his fault. 'I cried for the first time in my long racing career,' he added. Looking at this unusual behaviour, I thought I would have to do something to the machine for him. It was the first and the last time I saw him crying.

Last year [2002] I was involved in the development of the RC211V and this year I became an engineer exclusively for Nicky Hayden. During the off-season tests I didn't have much chance to talk to Daijiro. Yes, we were in different teams and there was a certain distance between us. I was a little sad about it but wished that I could work with him again in the future.

Yukiharu Kiyota (*left*) was Kato's chief mechanic in '99, the year when the NSR250 was greatly modified. Daijiro's input helped to improve the machine; he rode a 2000 prototype in the final race of the season. (*Takashi Akamatsu*)

OPPOSITE TOP: In '97 Daijiro won eight out of eleven races. This is his round 8 victory lap at Suzuka. (*Takashi Akamatsu*)

OPPOSITE BOTTOM: Toshiyuki Yamaji was Kato's chief mechanic in 1997 and '98. (*Takashi Akamatsu*)

Yukiharu Kiyota

HRC engineer

A present from Daijiro

In 1998 Daijiro did not achieve good results, and 'the issue of Daijiro' came up at HRC at the end of the year. I do not think HRC understood his talents properly at that time. On condition that he would get fired if he did not improve his performance, and that he could step up to the Grands Prix if he made a successful comeback, they decided to reshuffle the team staff and asked me to take care of Daijiro. I had been away from mainstream motorsport for a while and had little knowledge of him other than that they said he was a gifted rider.

Anyhow, I started by asking for another staff member to ensure a stable environment for him. It did not take long for me to learn he had an intuitive understanding of machines. His comments were straightforward and easy to comprehend. Once what he needed came out, what we needed to do for him became obvious. I believe Daijiro wanted to run round all the tracks at full throttle without slowing down his pace! In order to meet his wishes I called in an engine tuner and a machine designer, saying: 'Just look at him riding, and then make a machine that will fit him!' There might be little we could do, but I got him to join in and discuss what might be done.

Daijiro did not talk much, but he improved his lap times whenever the machine was changed successfully. No rider could be easier to work with than him, as his times indicated the machine's performance! In the first half of the season we kept losing out to (Naoki) Matsudo, a Yamaha rider, but a lot of trial and error started paying off in round 5 at Motegi. After three consecutive wins we came to believe we could extend this winning streak up to the final round.

Just before that round he had an opportunity to ride a 2000 prototype, which included all the work we had done over the year. As the test programme was focused on the existing machine we could spend only the last five minutes on the proto. He set 52.1s on lap 3. My hand holding the stopwatch was trembling. The official record at Motegi was at the 54s level while his unofficial best time was 53.5s. In just three laps he had reduced it by about 1.5s. I was astounded at the time as I knew how hard it was to reduce the time by even a tenth of a second. Time ran out that day, but if we had got one more lap in he might even have lapped at the 51s level.

I left it to Daijiro to choose the existing machine or the prototype for the race, and he picked the proto and took a win some 27s clear of the runner-up, Matsudo. But he could not become the champion. We all felt very sorry for him, and about not being able to help him score one more point, and cried. At the party just after the race we were all in the championship T-shirts we couldn't put on at the podium and we had a spree, waving the flag we were going to fly and saying: 'You are the champion whatever people may say.' Each staff member got a helmet and a Zero Halliburton case from him when he was leaving Japan to take part in the Grands Prix. All the staff who worked together that year still say it was the most enjoyable season.

I told Fabrizio (Cecchini) that Daijiro would certainly become a World Champion in one year, or two at the longest, when I saw him at HRC, but he didn't take it seriously. Afterwards he took time to come to see me and said: 'What you said is true.' I feel working with Daijiro set me a clear criterion for other riders. There have been no riders I would rate more highly than him.

At round 8 at Tsukuba in 1999 he took the chequered flag with a striking wheelie. Everybody was surprised at this and wondered what had happened to him as he barely expressed his emotions. Actually, his girlfriend had come to the track to see him racing for the first time, so we named the finish 'the Wheelie Goal with Love' and called her 'Victoria'. I wanted to tell this story at their wedding but I didn't have an opportunity to make a speech there.

1994–2002
Suzuka Eight Hour races

Daijiro showed his exceptional ability at riding big four-stroke machines during Suzuka Eight Hour endurance races. His first Eight Hour race was in 1994 when Daijiro, still a high school student, was teamed up with veteran rider Satoshi Tsujimoto. The race was stopped soon after the start, however, when one machine crashed and caught fire and the leading riders were engulfed in the flames. Daijiro was one of the victims. He was not injured, but his machine was badly damaged and he was forced to retire.

Daijiro and Terry Rymer were team-mates in 1995 and they finished 12th. In 1997 Daijiro was paired with Yuichi Takeda, a good friend since childhood, and their team manager was Kunimitsu Takahashi, the first Japanese Honda rider to win a GP in 1961. Daijiro took pole position but crashed during what was a rainy race, and they finished 9th.

Daijiro and Takeda challenged for the win again in '98, but their hopes were dashed by machine trouble. The bike just stopped at the 130R corner. Daijiro desperately pushed the machine back to the pits but it could not be restarted.

The following year Daijiro teamed up with Makoto Tamada. They battled

Suzuka Eight Hour race.
(Takashi Akumatsu)

with the pairing of Tady Okada and Alex Barros, but it suddenly started raining during Daijiro's stint and he crashed. In the end, Daijiro and Tamada finished in 8th position.

In 2000, Daijiro and Tohru Ukawa, who were both taking part in the GP 250cc class at that time, fought with Hitoyasu Izutsu and Akira Yanagawa, riding a Kawasaki. Daijiro and Ukawa won the race, getting prize money of 20 million yen. Until the year before, the prize money had been 10 million yen, but it was doubled because it was now the year 2000. Daijiro and Ukawa tried for a second consecutive win in 2001 but they were only able to finish fourth. The winners that year were Valentino Rossi and Colin Edwards riding a Honda VTR1000.

In 2002, Daijiro rode with Colin Edwards. Honda's plan that year was to reduce the number of pit stops from seven to six. Daijiro had a longer share of the riding than Edwards, and accomplished the task perfectly.

After Daijiro's death, in 2003, Manabu Kamata and Yukio Nukumi won the Suzuka Eight Hour race on a Honda and they dedicated the win to Daijiro.

Shinya Takeishi

Ex-All Japan Championship Superbike racer

The most unlikely rider to have an accident

My impression of Daijiro, who was my team-mate at HRC, was that he was always sleeping. In fact, he was able to get sound sleep just about anywhere. He was a 'free wheel' – simple, honest and natural – and he did not care what people thought. I used to think we should be more careful about our behaviour as factory riders, but he had the sort of character that made me feel he would be excused for minor things. He had good reflexes as well. When we trained together he achieved any programme very easily. He was so good at swimming, in particular, that no one could keep up with him.

As we competed in different classes we hardly ever raced together, but we did run in the Suzuka Eight Hour endurance races as rivals. Daijiro was fast even on a Superbike, so I followed him closely once to watch him. He was the type of rider who wouldn't try to overtake without a safety margin. I felt he was really focused. Although I made every effort to hunt him down his riding was risk free, allowing for good margins at any turns. I had the impression that he was the most unlikely rider to have an accident, so the one at Suzuka was absolutely impossible for me to understand. I can't believe it even now.

It was the first time I attended a rider's funeral. I had never been to one before as I felt I was going to be devastated, but in Daijiro's case I was determined to face reality, and so I went. However, Sete (Gibernau) still reminds me of him and makes me feel like he is alive and still racing somewhere.

Takuma Aoki

Ex-Grand Prix racer

We talked about the Daijiro Cup project

People say that Daijiro was a genius, but I guess perhaps he made an effort in secret where no one could see. He didn't talk much about what he did so I thought he was trying hard in a way I didn't know about. We are all the same and he is not so special, I thought at first. I did not think that any rider could ride that well just on pure talent alone.

I also enjoyed pocket bikes and stepped up from mini bikes to road racing in the same way he did, but we did not have many chances to do the same races because of our different ages.

Once, at the Suzuka Eight Hour endurance race, we were racing against each other. At the start Daijiro took the lead into the first corner, and at the S curves I overtook him and got back into first place. I could not accept being defeated by Daijiro because I had much more experience than him, as I was older by some years.

I wanted to do many more races with him, but I had injured myself so my wish could not come true.

Later, I became HRC's advisor and I had more opportunities to talk with him. Daijiro was not a very talkative person, but he always had a precise image of the riding that he wanted to achieve. He kept his distinctive riding style.

I am now organising a pocket bike school, and that's why he came to me for some advice about starting the Daijiro Cup in 2003. We were talking about coaching kids and we promised to co-operate together to promote racing. I thought if professional riders such as Daijiro could give some advice, children would have a better chance of racing. I promised to support him in the Daijiro Cup project, and this feeling won't ever change. Daijiro has gone, but he will never fade away.

Daijiro partnered Tohru Ukawa in the Suzuka Eight Hour in 2000 and '01, winning the first time and coming fourth on the second occasion. *(Takashi Akamatsu)*

Kunimitsu Takahashi

Ex-Grand Prix racer

I could understand him without exchanging words

It is more than 40 years since I took part in Grands Prix. I am 36 years older than Daijiro but, from the first time I met him, we understood each other well without exchanging words. It was during the 1997 Suzuka Eight Hour endurance race, when I was the team manager of Team Kunimitsu with HSC, that I met him for the first time. Daijiro and Yuichi Takeda were our riders for the race. Everyone in the team felt at home in the friendly atmosphere. The team ran the Eight Hour endurance race for two years, and then I asked him to become the team manager for our team – Masahiro Hasemi, Akira Iida and myself – which was taking part in the Motegi endurance race in 1999. He was always smiling and played his part admirably.

Nationality or riding style don't matter when you become friends. With some riders, like Luigi Taveri, whom I met while I was doing Grand Prix racing, I soon came to understand what he was like, as I did with Daijiro.

His way of riding was perfect. Obviously he had a natural gift, but he largely owed his World championship title to his parents. Motorcycles were the stuff of existence to him, as he started riding a pocket bike as a boy. He was of small stature, and I don't think he was good at English, but he became a champion in spite of those disadvantages. There must have been something that put him on top of the world. Maybe it was his aura that attracted people, for becoming World Champion isn't that easy.

I remained in a coma for about ten days after I fell and hit my head while riding in the Isle of Man TT in 1962. Luckily I came round and was able to ride again, so when I heard he'd crashed I believed he would recover as I did.

Tohru Ukawa

Moto GP racer

He had a unique aura, like no one else

It was at a pocket bike race at the All Japan Championships that I first met him. He stood out, riding so fast in white leathers and with the pick of machines.

He joined HRC after spending some time at Team Kotake, like me. We were completely different people, though we had many things in common.

My best memory was the Suzuka Eight Hour endurance race in 2000. We were partners, and I was confident of winning the race with him. On race day we had a superb victory, or so I thought, but Daijiro was fidgeting on the podium. I said to him: 'This is a festival held only once a year. We won this big event. You should enjoy it! We should take our leathers off!' We both undressed on the podium, and later got in trouble with our company. But there were no words to express that sort of joy.

In the press conference, we were asked: 'What would you do with a big prize of 20,000,000 yen?' I answered, 'Save it', but Daijiro said: 'Go out to party and spend it all.' You can see the difference between me and him from this story.

Daijiro's accident happened just in front of me. I rushed to the hospital after the race. Then I was asked to go and see him. He was in the ICU, but I did not want to see him just lying on the bed. The hardest moment was the time I saw him in his coffin the night before the funeral services, with his closed eyes. It was a time of quiet vigil over him, attended only by the small number of people who had been closest to him.

You know, when we race, we strongly believe we will never die. It was a big shock, the realisation that believing in immortality does not change reality. Why Daijiro? I am very sad and this pain will never disappear. He had a unique aura, like no one else, and he was a superman, not an average man. I thought Daijiro was a guy who could be a champion. He could rule the world.

During the '98 Suzuka 200km race weekend there was a presentation by Team Kunimitsu. Daijiro and Yuichi Takeda were there with team manager Kunimitsu Takahasi, a former Honda GP racer (*middle*). In '97 the pair finished 9th, but retired the following year with machine trouble. (*Takashi Akamatsu*)

OPPOSITE TOP: Daijiro won the 2000 Suzuka Eight Hour race with Tohru Ukawa. (*Takashi Akamatsu*)

OPPOSITE BOTTOM: In '01 Kato and Ukawa were keen to win the Suzuka Eight Hour for a second time. (*Takashi Akamatsu*)

Hitoyasu Izutsu

Ex-All Japan Superbike Champion

No one could fill in for Daijiro

Thinking of Daijiro reminds me of our battle during the 2000 Suzuka Eight Hour endurance race. I was a Kawasaki works rider and burning to defeat Honda. We chased each other, taking care of safety margins. I don't remember how many times each lap we switched places. I guess Daijiro, who was one up or much more than me in terms of overall ability, must have kept pace with me but I was really excited at the increasing enthusiasm of the crowd.

He came back from the Grands Prix just to run the final round of the 2000 All Japan Championship with his Superbike. The race was to determine whether I would be champion for the first time. I was having difficulty with injuries I had sustained from a crash in qualifying. During the race, Daijiro cheered me on with his fist in the air as he retired because of some mechanical failure. That gesture helped me sit up and put vigour into my race again. I couldn't win the race but I did realise my ambition of winning the championship. I was really glad about both his cheering and my series victory.

In his private life he was a bit clumsy. He scratched his yellow car on the wall of my apartment when he drove over to my place. I told him the car was touching but he left some clear yellow lines on that wall! Things like that made him more appealing. He was an outstanding rider on a motorcycle, but in his personal life there was something about him that made us feel like giving him a helping hand. Everyone liked him. I was someone who looked forward to going to the seaside or having barbecues with him.

After the accident people were talking about who was going to take his place. My name was included on the list of fill-ins as I had moved to Honda, but the job seemed too much of a burden for me. Who could ever have replaced him? No one could fill in for Daijiro. I realised he was a special rider.

Alex Barros

MotoGP racer

Daijiro was consistently fast, like Eddie Lawson

Daijiro was a really fast rider. He was consistently fast, like Eddie Lawson. It is easy to go fast for a lap but Daijiro was always fast so it was very hard for me to race against him. For instance, during the Eight Hour endurance race in '02, it started to rain towards the end and Daijiro was consistently fast even in the wet. I was chasing him and I wished it would rain harder, but it didn't so I could not catch up with Daijiro. Talking about rainy races, small riders such as Daijiro, Loris Capirossi and Marco Melandri are usually not so good in the rain. Maybe it is because their weight moves forward and the rear end starts to slide.

I remember Daijiro sleeping during an important staff meeting at Suzuka before the Eight Hour endurance race. It was the first time I met him. I was listening seriously to those who were giving us advice. Then I turned around and found Daijiro, who was sitting next to me, was sleeping and Yuichi Takeda was also fast asleep. At first Daijiro tried to open one eye, but soon he was sleeping deeply. He was such a nice guy. He was one of my friends in the paddock. Brazilians are cheerful but normally Japanese people are shy and melancholy. Daijiro, though, was a very easy and cheerful guy.

The accident at Suzuka was a shock to me. I have two children so I really feel sorry for Daijiro's family. But I only want to have happy memories of Daijiro. When somebody dies, you should only remember the happy times you spent with him or her. You shouldn't remember the accident. I want to remember the happy days I spent with Daijiro, and I also want to remember his superb riding.

Kato and Ukawa had a good fight with Hitoyasu Izutsu/Akira Yanagawa (Kawasaki) during the Suzuka Eight Hour in 2000.
(Takashi Akamatsu)

Colin Edwards

MotoGP racer

I threw my arms around Daijiro and gave him a big kiss

When I was told that I was going to race with Daijiro in the '02 Suzuka Eight Hour race, I was really looking forward to it. I knew Daijiro was fast on Superbike machinery as well as GP bikes. But I was much taller and heavier than him so, when I rode the bike with Daijiro's set-up, the rear suspension bottomed. Luckily, finding a compromise set-up was not a big problem for us.

Everything was all right until the final hour. Daijiro was leading the race but it started to rain and he didn't like rainy races. To make the situation even more tense Alex Barros, who is a rain-master, was catching up from behind. My heart was beating so much I could even hear it! Then I prayed: 'Please don't let it rain harder. I would give ten years of my life if this wish came true.' If it started to rain harder and Daijiro came into the pit I was ready to take over, so I sat there with my leathers on. However, the rain soon stopped and Daijiro was cool enough to get us through the crisis. When Daijiro took the chequered flag first I was so happy I felt like I was walking on air.

I have won the Suzuka Eight Hour race three times, in '96 with Noriyuki Haga, in '01 with Valentino Rossi and in '02 with Daijiro. The two previous races had been trouble free and we were cruising in the end. But the one with Daijiro was much more dramatic and I think, for me, it was the best Eight Hour race. When Daijiro came back after the winning run, I threw my arms around him and gave him a big kiss on his cheek.

I really miss Daijiro, but I will never forget the happy day when we were on top of the podium. I will never forget the moment when I threw my arms around Daijiro and kissed him.

Tomohiro Hasegawa

Shoei Helmet

Exhaustive work on helmet designs

Shoei is a company which provides promising young riders with helmets. We supplied Dai-chan with our products from the time he was a mini bike kid. Dai-chan was full of fun and it was pleasant for me to spend time with him.

Dai-chan was a real stickler with regard to helmet design. He had eyes on his helmet, as a trade mark. 'The right and left eyes are different, can you make this eye just 5mm longer?' he would say, and we complied with his request to make the eye longer. He also preferred the eyes to be bloodshot, that's why we added small red lines to them. Dai-chan checked and looked at details we couldn't see. He bothered about the angle of the number 74 too. He never gave me the OK unless he was perfectly satisfied with subtle modifications which were only visible to him.

He had many ideas for helmets, such as his request for the Suzuka Eight Hour endurance race: 'Prepare five helmets painted in different colours so that I can wear a different one at every rider change.' We accepted the challenge and accommodated his ideas and wishes because of his likable character.

My personal memory is that we had a really good time on a trip to Italy to visit Dainese in winter 1999. He was interested in wearing Dainese products, so I went to Italy with him as a translator and guide. Actually I took kind of a paid vacation for him. At the beginning Dainese had said they wouldn't support him at the All Japan Championship, but suddenly the president of the company gave Dai-chan the OK and we went to see him.

Daijiro's name seemed to be well known all over Italy too. Just two of us, on a boys' trip, but we enjoyed it very much and we also went a little way further, to Venice for some sightseeing and we took a lot of photos. It's a precious memory that I will never forget.

Daijiro's helmet design was his own idea. *(Takashi Akamatsu)*

OPPOSITE TOP: Daijiro, after winning the Suzuka Eight Hour in 2002. *(Tetsuya Yasukouchi)*

OPPOSITE BOTTOM: Colin Edwards kissing Daijiro on the podium after they won the Suzuka Eight Hour race in '02. *(Takashi Akamatsu)*

Tadahiko Taira

Ex-Grand Prix racer

He was one of the few born riders

There is a picture of Daijiro as a boy being held by me, but unfortunately I don't remember the moment. It was when he was with Team Kotake that I heard of him for the first time. They said an incredible rookie had emerged. Later on I had a chance to see him riding and thought his style was beautiful and natural. He rarely fell. Unlike me, an awkward rider, he was a born rider. I was interested in seeing how he would progress. He was able to manipulate any machine from a 250cc to an Eight Hour endurance bike. It was his natural talent which made that possible. There are few born riders, and as far as I know Freddie Spencer was one of them. Kenny Roberts reached that level by effort. According to Akiyasu Motohashi, my senior rider, Shiro Ito was also one of those born riders, though I have no personal acquaintance with him. Even in his first outing on a racing machine, after several months' absence, Ito was faster than Motohashi, who kept practising. Tetsuya Harada, a rival of Daijiro's, also looked like a born rider, but he was actually a hard worker, figuring out things like settings very carefully, and right to the point.

Daijiro's most impressive race was the Suzuka Eight Hour in 2002. Nobody knows what will happen in an endurance race until the riders finish. He led the field when it started raining, in the last half of the race. Under hard conditions, with a weary body, the deepening darkness and the rain he carried out his task perfectly. There are some riders who make mistakes when it comes to a showdown, but he was not that type of rider, and maybe that was more proof that he was a born rider.

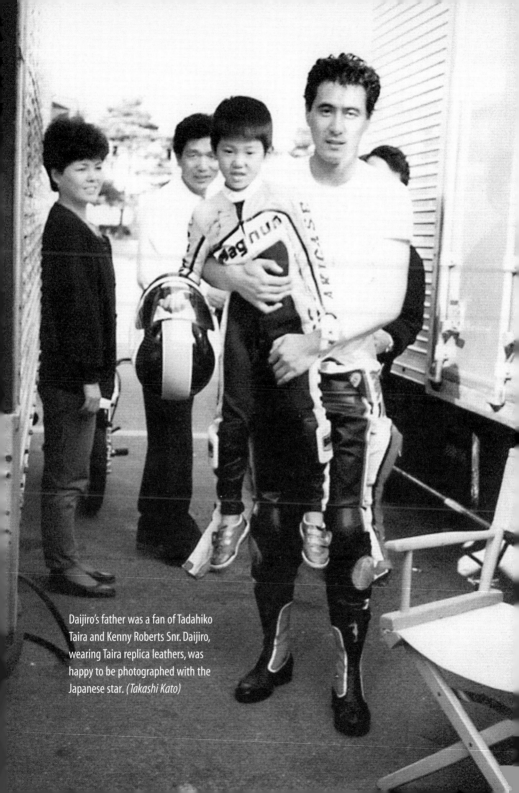

Daijiro's father was a fan of Tadahiko Taira and Kenny Roberts Snr. Daijiro, wearing Taira replica leathers, was happy to be photographed with the Japanese star. *(Takashi Kato)*

Daijro was consistently fast during the 2002 Suzuka Eight Hour race. *(Takashi Akamatsu)*

Manabu Kamata

HRC test rider

I wanted him to race under the same conditions as Rossi

Every time I went on an overseas test Daijiro was pleased to see me. I'll never forget his smile. He was always sleeping until just before the test started, but he was never late as somebody made sure to wake him up by cell phone. He was so imperturbable, he never panicked at all. Once we had a very limited time to change planes, but he was confident and said, 'Don't worry, I'm sure we will make it', while my heart was pounding. And I was surprised that we could always make it, as he'd expected. When he got drunk he would be limp, like an anaesthetised deer, but this insecure image was changing to a strong and reliable one as he got married and became a father.

For a magazine feature Daijiro and I went touring. When we had covered about 50km he said, 'I like it.' But how could he know about a long ride after just that short distance? I promised him we'd go for a really long ride together someday, but the promise was never fulfilled. I went on our annual seaside camping trip with some fellow riders in the summer of 2003, but I missed him so much and couldn't enjoy myself at all. 'What do I do without you?' I felt like crying.

I have another regret. Daijiro chose to join the satellite team in 2003, even though he could have chosen to ride in the factory team. He must have decided that after giving it much consideration, but I wanted him to become a factory rider, to race under the same conditions as Valentino Rossi.

In the 2003 Suzuka Eight Hour endurance race, which was held after his accident, I felt like Daijiro helped us win. When I stood on the podium I thought that he was supposed to be there. He enabled Honda to take seven consecutive wins in that race. We dedicated the victory to Daijiro.

Daijiro and Manabu Kamata enjoyed travelling together. *(Manabu Kamata)*

Manabu Kamata and Yukio Nukumi won the Suzuka Eight Hour in '03 and dedicated the win to Daijiro. *(Takashi Akamatsu)*

2003
The Japanese GP: lap 3

Before the start of the 2003 season, Daijiro said modestly: 'My aim now is to win a race on the RC211V.' However, winning the MotoGP World Championship was no longer merely a dream for Daijiro, it was a target. Many people were hoping that he would take the title in '03, or in '04 at the latest. Although he was silent on the subject, it seems that Daijiro himself must have had such a plan. He was doing very well in the off-season tests.

During the opening round, at Suzuka, it rained on Friday and Saturday. Daijiro never had a chance to become familiar with the newly configured chicane and qualified a disappointing 11th.

Race day itself, 6 April, was a clear day. Daijiro started from the middle group and was in sixth position after the second lap. He was trying to catch up to the leading group of Valentino Rossi, Max Biaggi and Loris Capirossi.

On lap 3 Daijiro went off the track after the 130R corner, just before the chicane. He crashed heavily into a barrier. He was given life-support treatment at the track's medical centre and then transferred to Mie Sogo hospital by helicopter. The doctors there told Daijiro's family that he was already brain dead. He fought for two weeks without recovering consciousness, but passed away on 20 April.

Funeral services were held on 20 and 21 April at Kaneiji Temple in Ueno. Many fans gathered, and also for the 'Farewell Daijiro Kato Ceremony', which was held on 18 May at Honda Motor headquarters in Tokyo.

On 25 April, Honda formed a committee of independent experts to investigate the cause of the accident. The outcome of the inquiry was reported on 28 November in Tokyo. Afterwards, Mr Suguru Kanazawa, the President of HRC, announced: 'The accident occurred in an extreme situation and it is difficult to determine the cause.'

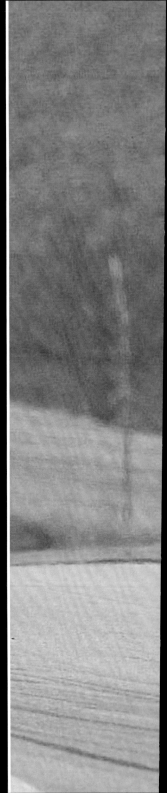

Off-season testing, 2003.
(Team Gresini)

Kiyoshi Kawashima

Supreme advisor at Honda Motor Co. Ltd

Daijiro was lucky to be with Team Gresini

It was at the Suzuka Eight Hour endurance race in 1994 that I noticed Daijiro for the first time. He ran the race with his team-mate, Satoshi Tsujimoto. 'How can they manage to share one machine with that big gap in their stature?' I wondered in admiration. When I was a team manager (in 1959–61) I focused on what rider to use for which race: Rider A for a race with elements of endurance and Rider B for a sprint race, as every racer has his strengths and weaknesses. In those days Luigi Taveri was known as an all-round rider. Daijiro also seemed to be one of the most gifted riders, able to cope with a wide range of categories from endurance to sprint races. I was happy to see such a good rider coming from Japan and looked forward to his future career.

Fausto Gresini, the team manager, and about five team staff attended the funeral service for Daijiro, although it was celebrated in a religion that was different from theirs. I was impressed by that. Many Japanese might think that the team manager should be responsible in a practical way for making the best of the races after an accident rather than attending the funeral, but such behaviour is essential to hold the team together and inspire the other riders. I thought Daijiro, who was really loved by Gresini and the team staff, was lucky to be with them.

Racing is at the root of racers' lives: it is not about what sponsors to get or which higher-ups are coming to watch the race. It's more about passion, about one's spirit. There are many people who forget this. I even thought of such things at the funeral. I was also impressed by the passion of the Japanese motorsport fans when I saw so many of them attending the farewell service at Honda's office headquarters.

Takeo Fukui

President and CEO of Honda Motor Co. Ltd

It was the dream of all Japanese manufacturers

As I was in Ohio from 1996 to 1999 (at Honda of America Manufacturing) it was at the Suzuka Eight Hour endurance race in '00 that I saw Daijiro riding for the first time. I was surprised to notice the big gap between his riding and his attitude while not racing. I also remember he hardly ever crashed. At the Eight Hour in '02 his riding was not affected by the rain which started in the latter stages of the race.

It has been Honda's dream to have a Japanese champion in the world's top class since we came back to the Grands Prix with the NR500 in 1979. There have been some Japanese riders who've taken the title in the 250s, or won a 500cc race, but no Japanese has taken the world's top class title. Daijiro was expected to do that. I wanted him to be the first Japanese MotoGP champion and a national hero, and that was also the dream of all the Japanese manufacturers.

He could have become a MotoGP champion. His intention was to accustom himself to the RC211V he'd switched to in the middle of the previous season, and then to aim for a World championship title the following year, I guess. I felt he could have done that. That's why we are very sorry.

We hope to follow his lead and promote the development of motorsport, expanding the basics of racing and offering opportunities for talented riders like Daijiro to develop their skills from childhood. There are no specific plans at the moment, but I will take it on as a Honda's mission, inspired by him, to build a solid foundation by making use of Suzuka and Motegi and to develop motorsport.

Before the start of the '03 season, Daijiro said: 'I have to win a race.' It was a dream that should have been accomplished.
(Shigeo Kibiki, SKP Inc.)

Suguru Kanazawa

President of HRC

A Japanese MotoGP champion is an ultimate goal

I first saw Dai-chan riding at the TI circuit in 1994. That was when he won an All Japan Championship race for the first time. There is a place where two consecutive left curves form one big curve and Dai-chan was treating these as one corner. I was amazed by his sliding technique there. The most impressive race was the '98 Japanese GP. The NSR250 was modified greatly that year and both Dai-chan and Ukawa could not achieve good lap times during off-season testing. But Dai-chan won the Japanese GP even though there were some disadvantages with his machine. Dai-chan was the only rider to win a 250cc race on the machine that year, both in GPs and the All Japan Championship races.

When I moved from HRC to Asaka R&D at the end of '98, riders, journalists and other staff organised a farewell party for me. Dai-chan gave me his leathers as a present. I couldn't keep them at my home, so I presented them to the Motegi Collection Hall, but I was really happy to receive this gift from Dai-chan. After I joined Honda I tried to keep some distance between myself and the riders, so I kept Dai-chan at a distance too, but he was always easy going and relaxed when talking to me.

To enable Dai-chan to win the MotoGP championship was one of our ultimate goals. In the past I'd believed Takuma Aoki could have become the first Japanese 500cc World Champion. We tried everything to help him achieve that goal, which is why we gave him the NSR500V first instead of the NSR500 in order to get him used to the category. But Takuma crashed and was injured. Then we were thinking, who could succeed with our dream? I myself was thinking about Daijiro then. I think he could have won the World Championship this year (2003), or the following year at the latest.

Shoji Tachikawa

HRC Repsol Honda team manager

He understood his situation by using mental pictures

Unlike many Japanese riders, Daijiro rode machines using his intuition. When he switched from 250cc bikes to Superbikes, he soon figured out how he should ride them, and at what speed he could pass other riders in the turns. It seemed like he understood his situation by using mental pictures in some way. That's why he was fast even right after switching to a new machine. The 2002 Czech GP, in which he rode the RC211V for the first time, is just one example. He usually looked a bit spaced out, but I think he inhabited his own world that he wouldn't share with others. The more he felt he couldn't explain in words, the less he spoke.

In 2001, Valentino Rossi won the title in the 500cc class and Daijiro did the same in 250s. I was highly delighted because I was a Honda team manager then. Daijiro was competing for the title with Tetsuya Harada, who did not finish several races due to mechanical failure, so we did our best to support Daijiro by maintaining the reliability of his machine. We all believed he would win the championship.

He showed extraordinary enthusiasm for the MotoGP World Championship in 2003. He even went to Saipan for physical training. I was worried, though, since that wasn't his style: I mean he used to be more relaxed and laid back. 'We have to be cautious with Daijiro. He looks so fragile this year, fragile like glass,' I said to somebody just before the Japanese GP. Yes, he looked as fragile as glass.

Before the start of the 2003 season Valentino Rossi named Daijiro as one of his strongest rivals.
(Team Gresini)

During the '03 Malaysia tests Kato put in some incredible times.
(Team Gresini)

Tadayuki Okada

Ex-HRC racer and former assistant manager of the GP team

Even against Rossi, Daijiro could have won the title

I have no experience of competing in the same races as Daijiro, except for the Suzuka Eight Hour endurance race. I'd already moved up to the 500cc class when Daijiro was a wild-card rider taking part in the 250 class in the 1996 Japanese GP. But I spent a lot of time with him, testing in the winter time and doing physical training, as well as keeping an eye on his riding. His riding style was beautiful, with strong use of his knees; in those days his riding was unique.

The best race of Daijiro's, as far as I can remember, was the Japanese GP in 1997. Daijiro was keeping Tetsuya Harada and Tohru Ukawa behind him and he won in the end. I thought Daijiro was a great guy.

When Daijiro was battling with Tetsuya for the championship in 2001, I was participating in the Superbike World Championship, so I could check Daijiro's riding more carefully than before by watching him on TV. I was convinced that Daijiro would become the World Champion that year.

Then I was sure he could become Moto GP champion this year (2003). I believed that, even against Rossi, he could have won the title. His riding technique was special, and he was better than any of the Japanese riders I have ever seen. He possessed something nobody had. That's why I feel sorry that he is no longer here with us.

Just after the accident at the Japanese GP, I also went to hospital at Yokkaichi and remained there for a while. I was thinking all the time, 'What happened to Daijiro? Why did it happen? Such a terrible accident…'

However, I do feel Daijiro is still nearby in some way. Makoto Tamada and I were kidding: 'Have you seen Dai-chan recently?' 'No, I haven't.' 'People are saying he is missing, just disappeared.'

Loris Capirossi

Ex-125cc and 250cc World Champion and MotoGP racer

I prayed every night after the accident

In '99, the year before Daijiro came to the Grands Prix, I was the rider for Team Gresini, so when I moved up to the 500cc class I often visited Team Gresini's pit box. When I went there, Daijiro was always sleeping in the corner. It was something like two o'clock in the afternoon, and he was deeply asleep and dreaming. Once a mechanic woke him up, though, he got on to his machine and started riding, and immediately he clocked very fast times. His riding was always clean and neat. It is not easy to win the World Championship in your second year, but Daijiro did that and I think he was a really talented rider.

Daijiro was my friend and his Italian was getting better so we talked in Italian. This year (2003) I am riding a Ducati. At the moment, its potential may be inferior to that of Japanese motorcycles, but it is fun to ride the bike. It would have been nice if Daijiro could have ridden a Ducati too. Usually, Italian riders ride Japanese machines but I want Japanese riders to ride Italian machines. If Daijiro were riding a Ducati, for sure the Italian press would have loved it. Daijiro was very popular among Italian journalists.

I was racing in the leading group during the Japanese GP so I didn't know about Daijiro's accident. When I heard about it, I worried a lot. Before he died, I prayed every night: 'Please God, don't let him die. Please give Daijiro back to us…'

In '03 Tady Okada was the assistant manager of the HRC GP team, and recognised Daijiro's exceptional talent. *(Team Gresini)*

OPPOSITE TOP: Daijiro being interviewed by DORNA. *(Team Gresini)*

OPPOSITE BOTTOM: A talk show was held at Suzuka on 5 April 2003. Loris Capirossi and Shinya Nakano took part along with Daijiro. *(Daijiro.net)*

Ryoichi Mori

Mechanic with Team Gresini

That day, Daijiro was smiling on the grid

I have been a mechanic with Team Gresini since 2000, the year I started to work with Daijiro. Daijiro was a rider with whom I felt comfortable working. Even though it was his first experience of joining a non-Japanese team, he acted quite naturally from the beginning. As Daijiro had a personality that attracted people around him, they easily got close to him.

He was very exact about settings, but he could also turn good lap times even when the bike was a bit off on setting. But above all, he wanted really fine settings. He requested what other riders did not ask for, or other riders did not mind very much about, but if I set it up as he liked, he would produce good results.

Daijiro was always free spirited. When he was competing for the championship with Harada in 2001, he was never nervous. It was his nature to feel free from strain.

In Daijiro's case he did not see anybody particular as a rival. He did not care who was fast or slow, he was pursuing his own riding style. Even when it was Rossi who was competing with him, it did not make any difference to Daijiro. All he was aiming for in his races was to achieve good results.

If you ask which was the race I enjoyed most, I would say every race. When he won or even when he lost, it was always a new story, which made me happy. If I fixed his machine without complaining when he crashed, he responded by achieving good results without saying anything. That was the sort of guy he was. Oh, just one time it was a regret for me that Daijiro crashed, when he was involved in Marco Melandri's crash at Motegi (the Pacific GP) in 2001.

At this year's Japanese GP (2003), I was the last man standing by him on the grid. He was so calm and relaxed. It was very similar to the atmosphere we had on the grid at Suzuka in 2001, the year he won the 250cc World Championship. Although it had rained during the week and his qualifying result was not so good, I had a hunch that he would win that day! He was so calm and he was ready for victory. No one but me knows that he kept looking at me and smiling for a long time after he closed his helmet visor, so I thought, 'Oh! For sure he will win today.'

After the accident, I could not go to the hospital immediately as I had to go back to the pit. I was waiting for news at the circuit. That night, I had to return to Saitama Prefecture to work on engine maintenance at HRC the next morning. Before leaving, I dropped in at the hospital in Yokkaichi. I saw Daijiro in CPU with the consent of his father. I said to him: 'I have to leave a little early but I will wait for you at HRC.' I was at the HRC factory in Belgium when I heard that he'd passed away. I could not believe it and I did not want to believe it. That was my feeling. Although I attended all the funeral services, I still cannot believe that it really happened. I still feel that he is walking around somewhere or watching from somewhere. Afterwards, it was really tough for me to go to the circuit, but I thought he would laugh at me if I did not move on. He knew my personality well.

I did not know if it would be this year or next year, but I was pretty sure Daijiro would become the MotoGP champion. I strongly believed that. I wanted to keep on working with him until he became the champion.

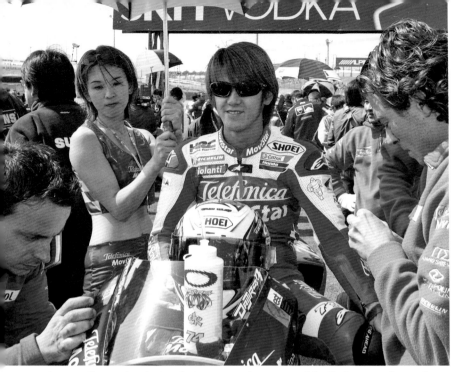

Japanese GP 2003: Ryoichi Mori, the Japanese mechanic, reported that 'Daijiro was smiling on the grid'. *(Team Gresini)*

Mori stayed with Daijiro on the grid until the start of the warm-up lap. *(Daijiro.net)*

It had rained on Friday and Saturday at the '03 Japanese GP. Daijiro qualified 11th and was not happy with his position. *(Vega International)*

Valentino Rossi

MotoGP and 500cc World Champion

I did have the chance of a great battle with Daijiro

Daijiro and I took part in different classes until 2002, and in that year I was riding a four-stroke RC211V from the beginning while Daijiro was on a two-stroke NSR500 until the middle of the season. Maybe people thought we hadn't had a chance to have a great battle, but that's not true! It was in '99 at Motegi, when I was riding the Aprilia 250 machine and Daijiro was a wild-card rider. It was raining and I was riding the Aprilia in the wet for the first time and I was a little bit cautious. Maybe Daijiro didn't like wet races either, so it was a fight for fifth place or so, but I remember we were battling for most of the race.

For sure, Daijiro was a very good rider. I didn't have much opportunity to talk to him, but when I went to Japan for testing in March this year (2003) we visited the HRC factory together. I really enjoyed the tour with Daijiro. He was such a nice guy, one of the best guys among the MotoGP riders.

I heard about the accident soon after the race finished. We couldn't get much information but I worried a lot. I heard the news of his death at my house in London. A friend of mine called and told me. I was shocked. Since the accident we are really working hard to improve safety at racetracks. I believe that it is the responsibility of all the riders.

Shortly after I heard the news of Daijiro's death I had to go to South Africa for the GP. It was really tough. When I was riding a motorcycle, though, it was better. I felt worse when I was doing normal things. I really wanted to race more with Daijiro. I think we could have become good rivals.

Takashi Kamata

Sports trainer

A training programme for the championship title

I have been a trainer at HRC since 1988, and started looking after Daijiro from the time he joined Team Kotake. The muscular strength of his legs was nearly four times as much as his weight, even at that time. I hope you will understand how amazing it is to hear that I usually tell athletes to build up muscle at least twice as strong as their weights. This shows how outstanding his innate physical ability was. His speed and power were excellent, but his stamina was not so good, although he looked exactly the same just after a race, even though other riders sweated and got out of breath. There was a secret skill in that. He worked his lower body pretty hard while riding so that he could minimise the use of his arms. There are some riders who fully stretch their arms for support as they enter turns, but Daijiro always kept his arms relaxed, and instead gripped the machine tightly with his knees on the exit of turns, balancing himself successfully.

He was top of the HRC riders in the test score for physical strength, and was second best overall if HRC's motocross riders were included. In the off season this year (2002–3) he and I made up our minds to commit ourselves to the World Championships, and I set up a training programme for him. Daijiro, who didn't use to train actively, started pushing himself very hard whenever possible. We were going ahead with the programme in a bid to win the championship this year, if possible, and if that was impossible, to take this season as a run-up to ensure the title for next year. In fact, we were going to do some training at Saipan, after the Japanese GP.

Kato and Rossi battled hard during the '99 Japanese GP at Motegi. *(Shigeo Kibiki, SKP Inc.)*

Nobuatsu Aoki

MotoGP racer

Daijiro's accident united all MotoGP riders

The first time I saw him was when Daijiro wore a Taira replica helmet at Akigase. He was just small kid, so it was as though only the helmet was moving on the bike. When we grew up we took part in the Suzuka Eight Hour endurance race. At that time I thought he would be a promising rider in the future.

When he won the 250cc World Championship title he was so powerful and he was an inspiration for riders trying to cope with the difficulty of consistently running good lap times. He had no faults, but was scrupulous and accurate. I just felt he was like a robot. I thought that when he rode the 500 in the MotoGP class he was going to ride it with his usual 'robot'-like perfection. But then I saw that he was human too, that it did not come easily for him either.

He suited a 250cc, but I guess he was handicapped by his body size with the bigger bike. However, I thought that he would overcome this problem and would be battling with Valentino Rossi in a short time.

The morning after Daijiro's accident I was stopped by Max Biaggi, in the lobby of the hotel. He said we, the MotoGP riders, were going to have a meeting all together. Many riders began to agree with Biaggi's idea. In South Africa we gathered, finally choosing five delegates from different countries: Rossi for Italy, Sete Gibernau for Spain, Kenny Roberts for America, Alex Barros for Brazil and me for Japan. We met to have a discussion on every Saturday in race week with a representative of Dorna (the promoter) and the FIM (Federation of International Motorcyclists) to examine circuit maps and so on. At their home GPs it was sometimes the case that riders were absent from the meeting because of their own busy schedules, but Rossi was never absent.

Bike performance is increasing and the circumstances surrounding us have changed, so we are seriously thinking about the meaning of 'safety'.

Carlo Merlini

Team Gresini staff member

I cried at the back of the pit box

I have so many memories of Daijiro that I can't stop talking once I start to talk about him. Team Gresini grew up with Daijiro and Daijiro grew up with us. The happiest race for me was the Malaysian GP in 2001, when Daijiro won the 250cc World Championship. Another good memory is the final race of '01. We decided we would dye our hair different colours. Fausto Gresini chose blond and one mechanic chose blue. Yellow was missing so, when Daijiro came back after the winning run, we put yellow spray on his hair.

Another great memory is Catalunya in '01, when a billboard was blown onto the track by the strong wind and the qualifying practice was stopped for ten minutes. During this period, Daijiro sat on a chair in the pit box and he was sleeping. Other riders were tense: they wanted to go for better grid positions. Practice resumed and a mechanic called Daijiro. He woke up and immediately he put in fantastic times.

After Daijiro died, Sete Gibernau said he didn't want to go to South Africa. The whole team was in shock. But we thought that Daijiro would want Sete to race so we went to South Africa. When Sete got the best time and took pole position, I ran to the back of the pit box and cried. We'd all had to withstand a tough three weeks after the accident and our emotions, which we tried to suppress, suddenly surfaced. When Sete came back after practice he said, 'Some special power pushed me.' Then Sete won the race next day and dedicated the win to Daijiro, who was with us in the sky. I cannot express how I felt when I saw Sete pointing up at the sky.

Daijiro and friends; Makoto Tamada is next to him. *(Daijiro.net)*

Daijiro talking about the forthcoming race, April 2003, with Tohru Ukawa beside him. *(Daijiro.net)*

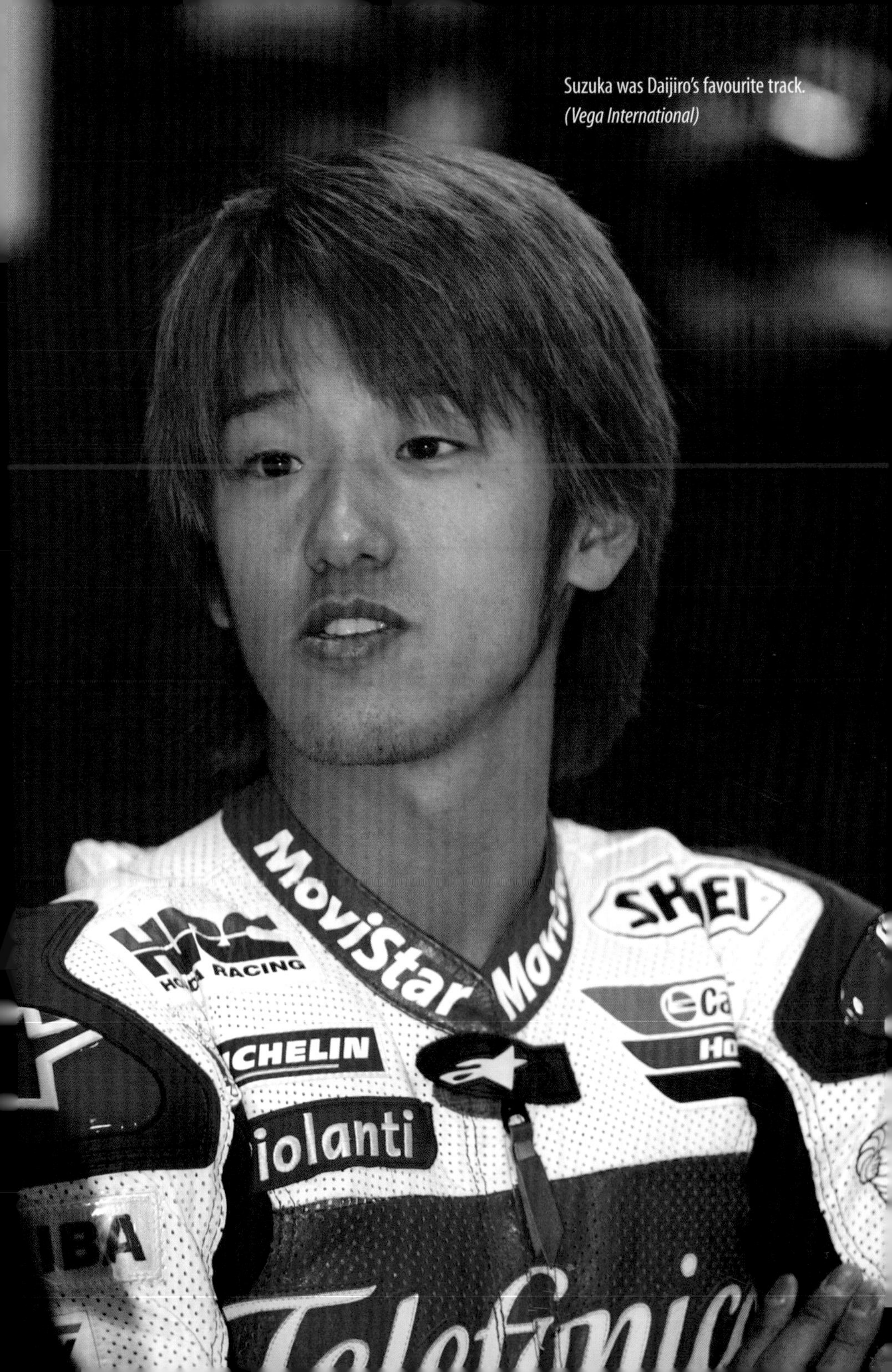

Suzuka was Daijiro's favourite track.
(Vega International)

Sete Gibernau

MotoGP racer

I had to win in South Africa

Dai-chan and I became team-mates for the first time this year (2003), but we got on well from the start. Dai-chan was an open-minded and easy-going person.

After the pre-season test at Catalunya I invited Dai-chan to my home in Barcelona. There we rode motorcycles together doing motocross, supermotard and the like. Dai-chan is usually very quiet but when we had a party on the last night, he got drunk and stood on the table. He started to take off his clothes and danced. It was so funny and everyone laughed a lot. Dai-chan had his favourite Spanish song called 'Asserap'. He sang in Spanish and his Spanish was perfect. During the Japanese GP weekend, he sang the song for me.

At Suzuka, during the MotoGP race, I made a good start but then fell back a few places. When I was catching up, I saw Dai-chan crash. I thought the race would be stopped but when I came back to the chicane on the next lap, nothing was left on the track, so I thought Dai-chan was OK and had walked to the track side. Still, there was something bothering me. I was thinking, maybe he is not OK… After the race, I heard about Dai-chan's condition. I don't know how to explain the feeling I had then. I was worried and sad but then I thought about his family. I was merely a new team-mate and it was gruelling for me, so what would his family feel?

After that, I told myself that Dai-chan would be OK. But I remember the moment when I heard that he had passed away. I thought of his family and his children. Just before the start of the Japanese GP, when I asked him, 'What is the name of your new-born daughter?' he said, 'I have a few names in my mind. Sete-san, please help me to decide the name.' So I said, 'OK, I will help you after the race.' I promised him to do that, you know…

Before the South African GP, I called the team and I said,' I can't come.' How could I race in that condition? The season was almost over for me. Then I thought about it again. Is hiding away forever the best solution, or should I do my best for Dai-chan's family? Which is the best…?

I couldn't believe that I won in South Africa. Everybody said that I won because Dai-chan was behind me, to support me, but I had to win that race. My team, Honda and everyone helped me and I won the race with everyone's support. The win was achieved by everyone's power and desire. It was the best way to show Dai-chan that we love him and we are always with him. That was the only thing we could do on that day. Of course I will go to his place one day. When I meet him there, I will tell him that I won at Welkom.

We don't know what death means. We don't know the truth and we fear death, but I am trying to think of it positively. I believe that members of my family who have passed away, and Dai-chan, will always stay with me and help me. Someday I will go over there and I don't want to see the rest of my family hiding away. I want to see them living positively and I will try to help them. I think Dai-chan is thinking the same.

Daijiro practised on dirt bikes as part of his training from the start of 2003. *(Daijiro.net)*

Daijiro Kato's farewell ceremony was held at Honda Motor's HQ on 18 May 2003 and many fans came along to say goodbye. *(Honda Motor Co. Ltd)*

OPPOSITE: During the South African GP, a '74' board was displayed alongside Gibernau's machine in the Team Gresini pit. *(Shigeo Kibiki, SKP Inc.)*

74
DAI-CHAN
YOU WILL BE IN OUR
HEARTS FOREVER
THANK YOU
15
HONDA
15

Daijiro and Sete became team-mates for the first time in 2003 and were getting on really well.
(*Team Gresini*)

OPPOSITE: Sete Gibernau won the South African GP and dedicated the victory to Daijiro.
(*Shigeo Kibiki, SKP Inc.*)

'Daijiro, we miss you'

He was famous before he became a full-time GP rider

Daijiro won the Japanese 250cc GPs in 1997 and '98 as a wild-card rider. As a result, he was famous abroad before he became a full-time GP racer. At that time, foreign journalists would often ask if Daijiro would be coming to Europe to compete full time in the World Championships.

He started riding full time in GPs in 2000 and finished third in the final 250cc standings. He won the championship the next year, after a superb fight with Tetsuya Harada.

In March '02, Daijiro received the Sports Merit Award from the Japanese Ministry of Education, Science and Culture. That year he moved up to the MotoGP class, riding the two-stroke NSR500 for the first half of the season. He then started to ride the RC211V, starting with the Czech GP in August, a race in which he finished second. Although he did not win a race in '02, all the media were expecting Daijiro to begin posing a threat to Valentino Rossi in the near future.

At the Japanese GP in 2003, a press conference was held in the press interview room after the accident and the room was filled with almost two hundred journalists. After his death, Daijiro was promoted to the MotoGP Hall of Fame, and his number 74 became a protected number, not to be used again by other riders. The ceremony for Daijiro joining the Hall of Fame was held at Motegi in '03, during the weekend of the Pacific GP. Daijiro was loved by all journalists for his honesty, charm and talent, and he is missed by everyone.

Daijiro's fairings. *(Daijiro.net)*

Michael Scott

British motorcycle journalist

We were fortunate to have Daijiro in our sport

There were two reasons why I followed Daijiro closely. The first was that I wrote a regular column in a Japanese motorcycle magazine called *Cycle Sounds*, and I followed Daijiro in the column. Another reason was that I was just interested in Daijiro. He was not only talented but also a unique and charming character rare in the macho world of motorcycle racing.

At first, Daijiro was an enigma to us Europeans. While he was racing in the 250cc class, all we knew was that his hobby was 'collecting shoes'. That was written on a profile sheet which Honda provided. One day, one of us asked Daijiro about it. He replied obtusely, 'I don't mind buying shoes.' He was an expert conversation stopper, and an extraordinary puzzle, with a perplexing twinkle in his eye. It was left to team boss Fausto Gresini to insist that, away from the track, Daijiro was warm, charming, and full of fun.

There are many Daijiro races that I remember well. One was his first win at the 1997 Japanese 250 GP. Another one is the 2000 French GP, when he crashed at the first corner on the first lap but remounted to pass two or three riders a lap, finishing sixth. The most impressive was the '02 Czech GP at Brno. It was his first time on the new V5 990cc RC211V, and I followed him closely for the whole weekend. A four-stroke rookie, he qualified second in front of Valentino Rossi, who had been riding the RC211V since the beginning of the season. Daijiro finished second in the race after the winner and Brno master, Max Biaggi.

He showed unbelievable potential then. It was sad that he did not have a chance to follow it through. I was lucky to be able to follow his progress in the short time he did have, and I believe we were all lucky to have such a genius in our sport.

Iain Mackay

Honda press officer

There is something common to great champions

I worked for Yamaha as a mechanic to Giacomo Agostini and Christian Sarron before becoming Honda press officer. After I started to work for Honda I was lucky enough to work with many great champions such as Freddie Spencer, Wayne Gardner, Mick Doohan and Valentino Rossi. There is something common to great champions such as Agostini and Spencer. That is, when they have a problem they don't seek somebody else's opinion, but they find the solution within themselves, along with their chief mechanic.

Another thing common to them is that they all have a quiet confidence in themselves. They don't usually take unnecessary risks. They all have a special presence, an aura about them. When riders line up on the grid and look at their rivals many lack strength and are beaten before the start. I guess Daijiro's rivals must have felt the same.

There was a kind of common behaviour between Spencer and Daijiro. Even when their qualifying times were not so good they didn't ask their mechanics, 'Who is the fastest?' All they asked was, 'What do I have to do (to take pole)?' But the most impressive thing about Daijiro was that he was a complete person inside. In other words, he didn't need the help of other people.

After the Japanese GP I went back to my office in Amsterdam and, when I arrived at Schipol airport, a gentleman, unknown to me, came up and asked: 'How is Daijiro Kato? Is he OK?' Maybe because I was wearing a Honda race jacket he could see that I worked for Honda. So many people called me and asked me to pass on 'Get well soon' wishes to Daijiro. I was really impressed by that.

When I think of Daijiro I don't think of him as a racer. I see a happy family man walking around the paddock with his wife and son. They were a complete unit, a happy smiling family. That's the way I prefer to remember Daijiro.

At a pre-event press conference in '02. *From left* Garry McCoy, Daijiro, Max Biaggi and Valentino Rossi. *(Shigeo Kibiki, SKP Inc.)*

Daijiro being presented with a Sports Merit award by Atsuko Toyama, Japanese Minister of Education, Science and Culture. *(Riding Sports magazine)*

OPPOSITE: Daijiro captured the attention of foreign photographers when he rode as a wild card. *(Rudi Moser)*

Satoshi Endo

GP journalist

If Rossi is a hatchet, Daijiro would be a samurai sword

During the 1998 off-season test at Phillip Island, in Australia, I was sitting on a hill, overlooking a turn coming up from the sea. It was a clear day and I was drinking water and sitting cross-legged. The NSR250 of that year was said to be a failure but Daijiro was rocketing out of the turn with it. I still clearly remember the scene. His throttle control from the braking point to the clipping point was so smooth and the acceleration from the exit of the turn was at an amazing pace. He was in a different class and it showed that he was a genius. If Rossi is a hatchet, Daijiro would be a samurai sword, which has the sharper edge. I was certain he was the fastest in the world. He was said to be in a slump that year, but it was due to the machine's limitations rather than those of the rider.

It seems to me there are two types of Grand Prix rider: those who come to the GPs by their own volition, and those who are awaited by everyone. Clearly, Daijiro was one of those few riders the world's racing fans had waited for. Everyone wondered why he hadn't come earlier. His late start in GPs gave all the more impact to his debut win. He made a great success as a Honda ace, and in his second year he became 250cc World Champion. As an athlete he had the kind of glitter that attracts people, a glitter defined by how that athlete can meet our expectations. In that sense he was the best racer I have known. The strong fighting spirit he showed at racetracks and his gentleness off the track were so different, and this attracted not only Japanese fans but also kids and adults from all over the world. He never spoke in English to the overseas media, but they accepted him. No one said, 'Hey, you must speak English!' to Daijiro. They all liked him. There was no Grand Prix rider like him. He was not a guy who would show off. Away from the track he seemed to enjoy being with his family and friends. I guessed his private life was nothing special, just ordinary like ours.

What Daijiro didn't have became obvious in 2002. If he had been taller and weighed more he would not have had so much trouble. He had been making up for these physical drawbacks with his unmatched throttle control and natural sense of speed. He was the best in the world in some ways, even compared to Valentino Rossi, Max Biaggi or Loris Capirossi. He had a lot of things that these three riders do not have. There are many riders who can race with these three guys but only a few can beat them. I believe Daijiro, who had something they did not, would have beaten them.

He might have needed more time, though. The 250cc class is a class where riders must try to use 100 per cent of the engine power, while in the case of MotoGP you must decide how much horsepower should be used. The skill and ability of each team make bigger differences in the MotoGP class. I wanted to see how the team would be working to improve its overall strength and overcome his disadvantages, because he was the only Japanese rider who could have defeated Rossi and reached the top.

Daijiro loved riding a motorcycle. Once he started riding he concentrated so hard on it, as if to say, 'Is there anybody who can go to the bathroom for me?' His heart was as tough as a diamond, and he was immune to superstitions, spells or pressure … sleeping in the pit until the last moment, then hearing that it's time to race he flicked a switch and came on to the grid. That was the style only a rider of genius could display. However, he was not someone who would attempt more than he could achieve. I thought he was the racer most unlikely to have an accident, and so was all the more shocked by it. The world's fans are still wondering why it happened.

Satoshi Endo (*middle*), the GP journalist, was a good friend of Kato's, and Youichi Ui treated Daijiro as a younger brother. *(Satoshi Endo)*

OPPOSITE: Daijiro crashed during the French GP in 2002 and was very angry with himself. *(Hidenobu Takeuchi)*

Hidenobu Takeuchi

GP photographer

Even Daijiro could have a grim look under his helmet

It was in 2000, when he began to take part regularly in the Grand Prix series, that I often got to talk to Daijiro. Some riders don't respond to me while they are wearing their helmets, but he never did that; he always answered me in the same manner, anytime and anywhere, without showing the slightest look of reluctance. There was no 'sorry, but it's not the time' with him.

Tetsuya Harada was more aware of him than Daijiro was of Tetsuya when the two competed for the championship title in 2001. To younger riders Tetsuya seemed really determined not to lose out, but he did appreciate Daijiro as a great rider. When he was defeated by Daijiro of course he felt sorry, but it looked like he felt he couldn't help it. Yes, Tetsuya appreciated Daijiro, and when Tetsuya was beaten by Daijiro he genuinely said 'Congratulations!' to him.

For his two years in the 250cc class Daijiro appeared rather laid back, but after he switched to an NSR500 he looked really different. He seemed to have some things on his mind, or to be having a hard time. One of the most impressive races for me was the one at Le Mans in 2002 (the French GP), in which Daijiro, riding the NSR500, fell just in front of me where I was taking pictures at the track side. I followed him as he walked away with his helmet on. Later I was surprised to see in the pictures that he had a grim look I hadn't noticed at the track and that he had never shown. Even Daijiro could have such a look. It was a great surprise to me.

Mat Oxley

British motorcycle journalist

Daijiro's riding – like art

Valentino Rossi likens his own riding style to a poem. I think Daijiro's riding was more like art – smooth, flowing and apparently effortless, betraying little outward sign of the rampant aggression required to win at the highest level. It was a beautiful style, a proper 250 technique, using devastatingly fast corner speed as his chief weapon. And it helped that HRC had developed its NSR250 around Daijiro, so the bike embraced him like a cocoon.

Daijiro's riding style worked just as well when he graduated to MotoGP in 2002, riding an NSR500 against the new and faster four-strokes. Although his NSR lacked speed against Rossi's RC211V, he very nearly beat the World Champion in only his third ride on the bike. And even if Dai-chan wasn't an instant success when he switched to four-stroke power later that season, it wasn't going to take him long to get the best out of the RCV.

Interestingly, recent developments in tyre technology have encouraged a crucial change in the way that successful premier-class stars ride their bikes. Corner speed is now the crucial weapon in any MotoGP rider's arsenal, which would have suited Dai-chan down to the ground.

Few experts doubted that Daijiro had the talent to become MotoGP World Champion. Rossi certainly feared this quiet, deep-thinking racer. During 2002 and 2003 the Italian talked a lot about Daijiro.

Daijiro's death was a tragedy, not just because he was a racer but also because he was a husband, a father and a son. I've been involved in motorcycles for many years and I've lost many friends to the sport that I love. There's no point in fooling oneself about the risks involved. You do this because you want to do this, and, however safe bike racing may become, you have to understand that the dangers will always be there.

The Australian GP in '02: what is Daijiro looking for? (*Team Gresini*)

Manuel Pecino

Spanish journalist

Daijiro's accident was the top news story in Spain

I knew Daijiro from the time he was racing in the All Japan Championship. We wrote articles about races in Japan and I heard that there was a talented young rider competing there. When he first raced in GPs, in Japan in 1996, I was looking forward to seeing him riding. At that time Daijiro had long hair and was like a boy from a Japanese manga (cartoon). He also resembled Norick (Norifumi Abe) a little. When I saw him riding for the first time, I was really surprised. I was sure he would become a great rider one day.

After he started taking part regularly in GPs he became like an iceman. He was cool and we couldn't read what he was thinking. Also, he rarely crashed. He was like a cyborg made at Honda R&D. He was not young when he started to come to Europe, but I understood why Honda had waited until 2000 to let Daijiro go there. Honda had finally unleashed their strongest weapon.

In Spain, Norick is very popular but Daijiro was popular too. In our magazine we showed the many sides of Daijiro, such as him sleeping with his helmet on. In Spain motorcycle racing is very popular, so on the day of Daijiro's accident it was the top news story on our national TV programme – not on the sports news but on ordinary news. We also received many letters and e-mails from our readers, enquiring about Daijiro's condition and asking us to send best wishes to his family. I know Sete Gibernau very well, since he is also Spanish like me. After Daijiro's death, before the South African GP, Sete was depressed. I told him: 'If you want to continue racing, you must go to South Africa, but if you are quitting you can stay at home mourning.'

Stefano Saragoni

Moto Sprint magazine, Italy

Many riders in Italy put '74' stickers on their bikes

I had been watching Daijiro since '98. That was when he won his second Japanese GP as a wild-card rider. If you are lucky you may be able to win a Grand Prix as a wild-card rider once, but you cannot win two consecutive races just based on luck. Daijiro was also fighting for the championship until the end of the season in 2000. It was his first full year and the change of environment was a lot for him to cope with. In '01, though, he was incredibly strong. He was perfect as a 250cc rider. I think we can also say that the NSR250 was tailor made for him.

His most impressive race was at Jerez in '02: Daijiro on the two-stroke NSR500 finished second to Valentino Rossi on the four-stroke RC211V, beating Tohru Ukawa on another RC211V. I will never forget that race. After switching to the RC211V at Brno the same year, he struggled a little. Maybe it was physically challenging as Daijiro was very small.

In Italy, motorcycle racers are heroes. MotoGP is the most popular sport after football and Formula One. Of course, more fans support Italian riders like Valentino Rossi and Max Biaggi, but Daijiro was also very popular. After the accident, news of Daijiro was on TV and in the newspapers, and many letters and e-mails came to the editorial office of Moto Sprint. There were also many street riders who put no. 74 stickers on their bikes. After his death, 'Via Daijiro' was built in Misano, where he used to live. In Italy, people loved Daijiro so much and we all remember him as a great racer.

Motorcycle racing is very popular in Spain. Daijiro's accident was the top news story on Spanish TV. (Team Gresini)

Daijiro won the 2001 Japanese 250cc race, making this Honda's 499th GP win.
(Shigeo Kibiki, SKP Inc.)

A Honda party held after the final 250 race of '01, in Rio: Dani Pedrosa sits on Daijiro's left, with Marco Melandri on the right. *(Hidenobu Takeuchi)*

Shigeo Kibiki

GP photographer

He kept riding in the rain

I still remember that his riding, as I saw it through my camera, was just so smooth. It was something that made me forget his small stature. He was an all-rounder who could manipulate every type of motorcycle from a 250cc to a Superbike for the Suzuka Eight Hour endurance race. There were only twelve rounds a year in 1973 when I started taking photos of the World GP Championship. Now we have sixteen rounds plus tests in the off season. I think it is now twice as hard for Grand Prix riders, who have to sacrifice almost everything of their lives.

One of Daijiro's most memorable races was the Suzuka Eight Hour in 2000. On top of the podium Daijiro and Tohru Ukawa, the winning pair, took off their leathers and everything until they were wearing only their underwear. I was surprised at this other side of Daijiro, as he had a quiet image.

Another race I remember was the Motegi round in 2001, at which he could have secured the 250 World Championship. Having got involved in Melandri's crash, Daijiro fell as well. This experience at Motegi, however, must have made him aware that winning the title was not that easy because he took the title with sweeping victories at the next two rounds, the Australian and Malaysian GPs.

Just before the Japanese GP I clearly sensed he was staking everything on taking the MotoGP championship title this year (2003). He kept riding in the rain on Friday and Saturday, even though he knew it would clear up on Sunday. He had never done that before. Maybe he was trying to overcome his reputation that 'Daijiro is no good in the rain'. I can never forget the scene.

Daijiro won the Malaysian GP and
took the 2001 World Championship:
he and the team were ecstatic.
(Hidenobu Takeuchi)

Jun Aoki

Chief editor of *Riding Sports*

I wish he could have gone up to the world stage earlier

The first time I thought Daijiro was outstanding was when I saw him racing at Tsukuba in 1993. He was taking part in the SP250 class of the Kanto Championship as a novice rider. His riding didn't look fast at all, but the lap times showed he was really fast and he won the race. I also heard about his heroic episode at Mase circuit when he was fighting against Haruchika Aoki and came into the pit after passing him, in order not to step up to the higher class the following year. One of the most impressive years for him was 1998 in the All Japan Championship. Since the machine was new that season the front tyre went into a slide a lot resulting in crashes, but he never complained about it to us. I still clearly remember him enduring this hard situation.

I wish he could have gone up to the world stage earlier. If he had had a hard time in GPs in 1998, he might have become the 250cc World Champion in 1999, and then the 500cc World Champion in 2000. He might have beaten Valentino Rossi in both the 250cc and the 500cc classes. There are no riders at the moment who can be a match for Rossi, are there? Maybe Daijiro had a clear image that someday he would become a World Champion in the top category. I don't know how many times he could have achieved it, but I believe he could have become the MotoGP champion this year (2003), or next.

After his accident *Riding Sports* received a lot of letters from its readers. Some wrote that it was the first time they'd bought racing magazines, and some wrote they were made aware again that they were fans of Daijiro. The July issue of 2003 featuring him was immediately sold out and we were surprised at how much interest people had in Daijiro.

Takanao Tsubouchi

Head of Vega International

Tetsuya was a good example for Daijiro

Maybe I was one of those who didn't appreciate Daijiro until the last moment. I believed that Tetsuya would beat him and become the World Champion in 2001 until just before the opening round of the season. I have seen several riders who were said to be geniuses, and one of them was Tetsuya Harada. There were only a few riders who were better than Tetsuya. If I had to name them, maybe only Max Biaggi would be included. I was supporting Tetsuya that year, as I knew he was having a hard time at Aprilia, but halfway through that season I thought Daijiro might possibly outrun him.

I had known of Daijiro since he took the title at the All Japan Championship but I didn't cover that series as I was keeping track of the Grand Prix races. I got the impression at first that he was not very rider-like, but laid back and relaxed, as described by many people. He appeared to make himself look like that to strangers. I gradually came to be aware he had something inside him that was different from the image he wanted to project.

I think it was really good for him to have competed with Tetsuya. The mentality is different between Japanese and foreigners, and so we are apt to take any differences for granted in dealing with people from abroad. Tetsuya is Japanese so maybe Daijiro could learn more from him than he could from foreign riders. Tetsuya was a good example for him.

I believe Daijiro could have become the MotoGP champion. I wish they would have let him ride the RC211V immediately after he took the 250cc title, as being held in suspense can be harmful to a rider's growth. You know, Wayne Rainey used to be the same when he raced a 250cc bike.

Daijiro signing autographs during the '02 Honda Thanks Day for fans. *(Daijiro.net)*

The legendary Giacomo Agostini (*second from left*) came along to support Daijiro. *(Team Gresini)*

1300 fans gathered at Motegi on 5 October 2003 to commemorate Daijiro. *(Shinichi Fukushima)*

On 4 October 2003 Daijiro's name was added to the MotoGP Hall of Fame. *From left* Angel Nieto, Kenny Roberts Snr, Mick Doohan, Takashi Kato (Daijiro's father), Fausto Gresini, Suguru Kanazawa (HRC President), Carmelo Espeleta (DORNA). *(Takashi Akamatsu)*

Tsuyoshi Chiwa

Associate editor of *Moto Champ* magazine

Daijiro was good on the balance beam

I met Daijiro when we were racing mini bikes at Akigase. I am eight years older than him, and the class I ran in was different from what he did, but since we found we were both from Kanto area we got to talk to each other when we went to Kansai. After that, I joined Sanei Publishing Inc. and quit racing, but he moved up to road racing.

It was at the 1996 Japanese GP in which he ran as a wild card that we renewed our acquaintance. I covered him throughout the event for a feature for *Moto Champ*. Of course I kept paying attention to him after that, and was just amazed that he stepped up to the GPs and maintained his place there. He treated me like he had before, even when he became famous, and he invited me to come to his team suite at some races, like the Suzuka Eight Hour endurance race. He remained the same warm person he had always been. During the off season in 2000 he called and asked me to go to a driving school with him to get a licence for motorcycles over 400cc. The challenge was covered by *Moto Champ* and we went to the Rainbow Motor School located in Wako City in Saitama. We had the smaller motorcycle licence already so we were exempt from the written test, and we passed the practical exam with the minimum twelve hours of lessons. Daijiro was not good at the 'slalom' (a course with obstacles of pylons, one of the tests required for the licence) but he was good on the balance beam. We were both aggressive and couldn't stand losing, so we competed over how short a distance we could stop, making use of two straight lines for testing safe braking, or how long we could stand on the balance beam. Our instructor knew Daijiro was a famous rider. We got our licences successfully and were going to take a long ride together someday, but that didn't happen. I feel he is still around somewhere.

During the off season in 2000 Daijiro went along to a riding school with his former rival and friend, Tsuyoshi Chiwa, to get a licence for riding motorcycles over 400cc. *(Moto Champ, Guts Ishimatsu)*

Daijiro and Chiwa were great rivals; Daijiro was good on the balance beam. *(Moto Champ, Guts Ishimatsu)*

2003

Wins dedicated to Daijiro

After Daijiro's accident, his family received 'Get well soon' letters, e-mails and Senbazuru (traditional Japanese origami paper cranes, to send wishes for a quick recovery) from all over the world. His family stayed at the hospital, praying that he would get better, and his friends were at hotels near the hospital, visiting him daily, but their hopes were never realised. Everyone was devastated when he died, but some of them just had to face the reality of the situation and continue with their own racing careers.

On 20 April, the Honda Formula One staff at the San Marino car GP were wearing black armbands. On 27 April Daijiro's team-mate Sete Gibernau, with number 74 badges on both his leathers and his RC211V, won the South African GP, a victory which brought many people to tears. On the same day, in Japan, Satoshi Motoyama, who was like an older brother to Daijiro, won the Formula Nippon car race at the Mine racetrack.

On 11 May, Chojun Kameya, a cousin of Daijiro's, won the All Japan Championship 250cc race at Tsukuba. Kameya had been taking part in the class for eight years, but this was his first win. Takahisa Fujinami won the World Trials Championship round on that day and Naoki Serizawa won a race in the All Japan Motocross Championship. All of these people were friends of Daijiro, and all dedicated their victories to him. In 2003 Yuichi Takeda switched to car racing and won the Vitz Championship, while Motoyama won both the Formula Nippon and All Japan GT Championships.

A number 74 sticker was on everyone's machine, helmet and leathers, both in the MotoGP class and in other categories and classes of motorsport. Following Daijiro's death, people in the sport grew more conscious of safety standards, and safety committees were formed by riders and drivers. Nowadays, technological development is swift, and the motorsport world is changing rapidly. Riders and drivers have to focus more on safety issues, to protect themselves after Daijiro's sad demise.

Daijiro was warm and gentle.
(Team Gresini)

Norifumi Abe

MotoGP racer

No. 1 rival

I met Daijiro for the first time at Akigase when I was a seventh grader and he was a sixth grader. I was shocked that Dai-chan and the other boys were riding very fast on their bikes. I was amazed at the difference in the level of riding between myself and Dai-chan. After we became friendly I often went to his house to stay, and we travelled to domestic races, that's why we always spent time together at the weekend. We were like brothers. No, we were more than brothers, because we were always together.

Dai-chan was the fastest rider among us: 'Catch him up! Overtake him!' We all competed. All of us were brats, and always getting into trouble, but it was mischief that was exciting and made my heart beat quickly. Anyway, Dai-chan was the top rider and acted like our boss; I wanted to be faster and to become the boss like him.

I remember very well a four-hour endurance race which we entered. I was given a warning by Dai-chan, 'No crash', because I had crashed many times before. However, he was the first rider and he crashed in the race. Dai-chan came back immediately after the crash and said 'sorry' to me. Then we moved up the field, and pushed very hard, and we finally won. Well, we really felt satisfaction at this and shouted for joy: 'Yeah!! We made it!'

If it had not been for the three-year period at Akigase, I would not have become a Grand Prix rider. I had friends there and we tried hard together. We improved our racing skills by competing – 'I wanna be faster',' I don't want to be defeated.' If I had practised by myself, I would never have become faster. There were always other boys to ride with, that's why I am here now.

At the age of 16 I went to America, and I debuted in the road race series there, so we had few opportunities to see each other. But for me, Dai-chan was always the no. 1 rival.

Well, I was lucky to go to Grand Prix racing early, but he was not. I used to wonder why he did not go to the GPs although he was so fast. Finally, Dai-chan came to the GPs, and we were able to race in the same class from 2002. At the French round we had a chance to battle hard, and I did not want to be defeated. It was really fun for me, like our mini bike fights.

For me, Dai-chan was different from other riders, because he was my rival, the number one guy I did not want to lose to. It's hard to explain why I feel this way, but I wanted to be able to look back on our years together peacefully when we were old and he would not be a rival anymore. I wanted to talk about many things with him. We aimed for the top in the same way, so there are things only we know.

After the accident I worried about his condition, but I had to go to Europe for a test, so I was away. That day, I had a pain in my heart. Then I felt uneasy, and I could not sleep. I wondered if something might have happened to Dai-chan. Next day, I received word that he had passed away. I tried to hold back my tears in front of my team staff, but I could not stop myself from crying and I could not continue testing the bike. I decided to go back to Japan to attend the funeral services. When I went to bow to his family, Dai-chan's parents said to me, 'Be careful.' They had taken care of me like I was Dai-chan's brother in the old days, and at their words large tears trickled down my cheeks again.

It is not possible for me to accept his death. I cannot bear it, it's too hard and very painful that such a terrible thing happened to Dai-chan, a rider who would push to the limit but, at the same time, would avoid any danger. For a rider, winning races confirms your feeling of being alive, but we know death is nearby. However, we must keep riding and believing 'I am OK', even though I was confronted by such a hard reality.

© Daijiro Kato

In '02, Daijiro moved up to the MotoGP class. *(Team Gresini)*

Shingo Yanagimoto

Daijiro's mechanic and personal manager

He was not the sort who sacrificed everything to win

I was holding a stopwatch for the track tests with Team Kotake. Daijiro was said to be a match for Haruchika Aoki, but I did not take that seriously. However, I soon realised he was. All of HRS Kyushu, Honda's test course of less than 2km, can be seen at a glance. This 15-year-old youngster soon set a new record there, with a perfect way of riding that was completely the same as the one in his MotoGP period. I was working for Kotake while racing myself and one day I was told to work as a mechanic for Daijiro. Driving him to and from the airport and warming up his machine was my job. He made a clear sweep at Kyushu and became champion in three classes without any difficulty. Fukumi Kotake, the team owner, did not allow riders to modify their machines based on his principle that riders should not think about winning with better equipment than others.

I also worked with Akira Yanagawa and Tohru Ukawa, who are both world-level riders. Yanagawa put track maps on the wall of his bathroom, and Ukawa used to devour circuit maps as well, but I never saw Daijiro doing such things, he was always sleeping instead. He was, however, a rider who made every effort at the track without running slowly or waiting for anybody.

At the end of 1993 I asked Mr Kotake for his approval to quit racing myself and to work exclusively for Daijiro. I told him I didn't need any salary, because I thought I could aim for the World Championships with him. The first year, 1994, was a challenging year for us. We were working very hard, running at tracks we had never experienced. At Suzuka, for example, we trimmed the footpegs of the machine for easier cornering. That misguided effort was due entirely to my poor skills. But he won there! There were a lot of factory machines taking part in the 250cc class in 1994, but I believe he could have become a series champion even with a production RS250 if a skilled and experienced mechanic had been working for him.

When Daijiro was set to join HRC in 1997 he asked me to come along, but I stayed at Kotake to brush up my skills. Parting with him left a great void in my life: I was like a guy who had lost his loved one. He asked me to come with him again when he was set to run at the GPs in 2000, but I couldn't due to my tight schedule. When he became 250cc World Champion in 2001 I thought I could have been in the circle of those sharing the victory with him and I envied them. Daijiro asked me to work with him every year, not because I was an excellent mechanic but probably because he wanted someone close to him. He had been competing since childhood, with a lot of people around him, and I guess he probably preferred the atmosphere in the paddock to the racing itself. He was not the sort of rider that sacrifices everything to win.

I managed to sort out my schedule so I could work with him at last in 2003, but what he needed most was a manager. I hesitated about giving up my mechanic's tools, but finally took on the job, hoping that looking at a team from the outside would be a good experience. During the off-season tests, when I went along with him, he set a new lap record after only two or three laps of riding the machine with its initial set-up. From there his own set-up kicked in. He seemed to be having trouble, with a lot of pit stops and a choice of piles of tyres, but all he could do was take time with the set-up and then he would have full control of the RC211V, which is the best machine in the world.

We used to talk a lot about his future, after retirement, and we were dreaming of different things besides racing. But our immediate goal was for him to be a MotoGP champion. I was quite certain he would become the MotoGP World Champion.

Shingo Yanagimoto, a friend of Daijiro's since 1993, exchanges a joke with him on the grid at the TI circuit in '96. *(Takashi Akamatsu)*

Makoto Tamada

MotoGP racer

Daijiro's way of riding has been my ideal

Daijiro started racing at Team Kotake earlier than I did. He was very fast from the beginning. I called him 'an invincible little boy' behind his back, as I didn't know him well, but he certainly was quite a rider. I thought I wouldn't be able to catch up with him with a half-hearted attitude, so I moved from my parents' place in Ehime to Kumamoto to create the sort of environment where I could commit myself to racing. But Daijiro was way ahead of me and I couldn't compete with him in the All Japan 250cc class.

When Daijiro won a race in the 1997 All Japan GP250 series he was running in temporarily, I got goose bumps. He passed both Tetsuya Harada and Tohru Ukawa cleanly to get through the final turn. Since then his way of riding has been my ideal – quick to bring his motorcycle back upright, with a beautiful riding style at corner exits; his control, tactics, etc. … everything was great. Valentino Rossi doesn't seem really formidable. I still believe the fastest rider in the world was Daijiro. Defeating him someday had been my aim. When I was not going well, he was the one who dared say to me: 'You're so slow Tama-yan!' Obviously I got annoyed at that, but usually I hit it off with him very well. He used to send me e-mails or call me about going shopping or eating out together. I was excited to be paired with him in the 1999 Suzuka Eight Hour endurance race. Daijiro was very fast in qualifying, and maintained the pace to enjoy a comfortable lead in the race. I was battling Alex Barros, aiming for victory. But it started raining and he fell. We didn't give up, though, and managed to take the chequered flag in eighth. I wanted to be his partner again and stand on the podium at the Eight Hour race, but the opportunity did not arise.

After I joined the Honda works team in 2001 we spent more time together.

I always found myself being playful with him – we used to mess about and tickle each other. I can tell you a secret. Just before the Eight Hour in 2001 I was carrying him on my back, in fun, in the parking lot of Suzuka circuit, and he fell as a car was backing up. He got his foot run over. Tadayuki Okada, who witnessed the scene, came rushing over, saying, 'Watch out!' and he hit me fair and square on the head. It was really painful, but there was no time for me to complain about it because Daijiro was crying out 'It hurts!', holding his foot. I turned pale. I called a doctor at once, and he assured us nothing was wrong. For the race Daijiro was teamed with Ukawa, and I was the reserve rider. They finished in fourth, but nothing went well. We both thought we weren't going to act around like that with each other any more, but things did not really change, I guess. When I was finally set to run in the GPs, in 2003, we were planning to build 'paradise' overseas. What do I mean? Well, it's hard to explain, but we were just going to have some more fun together.

And yet suddenly he is gone. I was always riding behind him, looking at his back. It's not fair! My chance to get ahead of him has been lost forever. You bastard! I still get angry thinking about it. I didn't cry at the hospital or at his funeral service because I couldn't believe he had passed away. When I was waiting in the pit, for the start of the South African race, I happened to look up at the monitor and there was a huge picture of Daijiro – something like his commemoration programme was on the air. I couldn't take my eyes away from it, even though I knew I should concentrate on racing. Tears were welling up. I cried aloud with my helmet on. Without Daijiro I could not have come this far. He helped me get to where I am now. Thank you, Daijiro. I want to say thank you directly to him.

'Dai-chan's way of riding was my ideal,' said Makoto Tamada. The pair were good friends. *(Takashi Akamatsu)*

Haruchika Aoki

Ex-125cc World Champion

I believe he could have become a MotoGP champion

I met Daijiro when I was in the pocket bike class. As we fought a lot of races I don't really remember who won or lost in what races but I still clearly remember I had some enjoyable times with him, Yuichi Takeda and Chojun Kameya when I went to Akigase circuit. I spent much more time with my pocket bike friends than my friends at school. These Akigase riders also came over to Haruna, our home course. I am the youngest of three brothers, and almost all my bikes were handed down from my brothers, while his were always shiny brand-new ones. I envied him a little.

Talking of Daijiro, I also remember a local 125cc race in 1992 at Mase circuit where we were disputing victory. He passed me with five laps to go and then pitted, but never came out again. That really pissed me off. I knew in order to run the Suzuka Four Hour race in 1993 he didn't want to come up to the All Japan Championship, but that's so unfair! I thought I was going to really defeat him properly someday.

Unfortunately, though, I was no match for Daijiro. I came to fully appreciate his talents during the 1998 All Japan GP250 series where I was riding the same machine as him. The Honda 250s of that year were difficult to handle. During the off season, I'd already felt that winning with such a bike would be extremely difficult. But he won with it! No matter how familiar he was with Suzuka, it was amazing. I watched the videotaped race repeatedly at home and was so impressed by my rival. He turned out to be the only rider in the world in 1998 who won in the 250cc class with a Honda.

It took him some time to come to the GPs, but once he made it, he did quite well there. I am confident I could defeat Valentino Rossi under the same conditions – I couldn't keep racing if I didn't think so, and I am sure every rider thinks the same way. I could read Rossi's next move, but in Daijiro's case I couldn't tell what approach he would take next. Maybe he had a unique talent that nobody else had. I believe he could have become a MotoGP champion.

In private Daijiro and I were very close family friends. After I came back to GPs in 2001 we increasingly spent more time together and finally we were almost always together. We used to barbecue or eat out together. When we had time we used to play games in his motorhome. He was no good at games. He didn't display any frustration when he lost, but perhaps he was frustrated. He once brought a game and asked me to play with him – he said he had hardly tried it, but he must have practised it a lot. Of course he won. I felt he couldn't stand losing.

When the accident happened I was at Suzuka and rushed to the hospital. I cried when I heard from a doctor I knew that he was in a critical condition. I was told to go home, but I spent the night in the lobby with Satoshi Tsujimoto. I prayed, hoped and believed in his recovery, but he went away. I couldn't stop crying at his wake service or at the funeral. Looking at smoke rising from the crematorium I cried out, 'Where are you going?' I thought I had no more tears to shed, but I still feel like crying when I remember him.

Daijiro won the Japanese GP in '98 but didn't do so well in the All Japan Championship that year. *(Takashi Akamatsu)*

Noriyuki Haga

World Superbike Championship racer

I looked forward to battling with him

Daijiro Kato, Chojun Kameya, Yuichi Takeda and Norifumi Abe were all based at Akigase circuit, located in eastern Japan, while Kensuke, my older brother, and I were from Nagoya, in western Japan, but we clashed with each other on mini bikes at different tracks. We won some and lost some. It was a lot of fun to chase or to be chased by these guys. Everyone, who was too young to think about their future too seriously, competed in a friendly atmosphere, enjoying every single moment. Several years later I met Daijiro again at the track, but I hardly ever raced against him due to the different classes and different series. It was only after we both began to race in Europe and became fathers that we often dined out together with our wives and kids. What we talked about was usually our kids, as we both loved them so much and wanted to be good fathers.

I felt we both respected one another as riders, but I never saw him as a rider of genius or a rival, because it had been natural for us to race together since our childhood. When I came to race him on the same stage at last, in 2003, I was expecting to run exciting races with him. In fact, I looked forward to battling with him as we did in the old days. But suddenly he was gone. It was like throwing cold water on my expectations. 'What's going on?' I still feel like complaining to him.

My brother has been in a wheelchair since a crash during a test, but he says this did not happen because he was racing. You cannot be free from danger even when you are walking down the street. Of course motorsport can be dangerous, but I won't quit racing as I couldn't do anything else, and neither would Daijiro. He would have kept running if he had been placed in the same situation as I am now in. I think all we can do is to take everything as it comes and keep running.

Katsuaki Fujiwara

Supersport World Championship racer

My close friends

What an amazing rider he was to manage a big bike with such a small build! It's maybe hard for a rider of less than 60kg to handle that big a bike but actually he only weighed about 50kg. A superb sense of balance must have allowed him to ride it so beautifully. I think Daijiro was a rider of genius.

I became close to him after both of us got married. As our wives are friends the families saw a lot of each other in Europe. When he found time, he came over to cheer me from his place in Misano. We used to go to good seafood restaurants, joined sometimes by Noriyuki Haga and Haruchika Aoki.

I was asked by Haruchika to come and watch the Assen GP in 2002. At night we played a game, calling each other by nicknames. Daijiro was called 'miserable' as he was no good in the rain. Haruchika was 'small light bulb' as he put on a weird knitted hat. I was 'little black Sambo' as I am dark and suntanned. When Makoto Tamada joined the game he was called 'Tamada bug'. Everyone enjoyed the game, laughing very loudly. I like fishing, and we were going to have a fishing team with Daijiro and Tamada – they were so close, they used to put chewing gum in one another's hair or have fights. It was fun to spend time with them. We were as close in the off season when we sat around a table to have dinner.

On that day Haruchika called me, crying, and I learned about Daijiro's accident. I said: 'Don't cry, he'll survive' because I believed he'd never leave his family or his friends. I want to ask him, 'Hey, what's going on with you? What really happened?'

REPSOL YPF
REPSOL YPF
1
Fortuna
MoviStar
Telefonica MoviSta

Daijiro became the 250 World Champion in 2001 and was proud to put the no. 1 sticker on his machine. *(Team Gresini)*

Naoki Hattori

Car racer

I became a motorcycle fan because of Daijiro

I was introduced to Dai-chan and Yuichi Takeda by Satoshi Motoyama at Suzuka.'These are my kids,' he joked.They were small, cute and young, and they really looked like kids.

Later I came back from the USA and moved into Minato-ward, at the same time as Dai-chan. Motoyama and Wakisaka were car racers and lived in the same apartment, and many friends from the car and motorcycle racing worlds often visited us. It was like we were back at school, because we used to gather in someone's house and play TV games or have something to eat and drink.

We also enjoyed racing karts together. Yuichi had a better sense of driving on four wheels than Dai-chan. But Dai-chan was a light weight, so he spun out a lot in turns. He used to drive too fast and too deep into the corners, and run out wide off the track. It used to make me nervous, but it was so much fun.

I was only interested in car racing before I met Dai-chan. I was not all that interested in motorcycle racing before, but now I have become totally fascinated by it and I am a big fan. I was surprised that, at the circuit, his personality was absolutely different from his usual self.

The biggest surprise for me happened in summer of 2000. At midnight I was called by Motoyama because Dai-chan was going to make a serious big announcement. I went to Motoyama's flat with my pyjamas on, and then Dai-chan said:'I'm going to register our marriage tomorrow and we're having a baby!' I was really surprised! He was a man of integrity, but he was also really cool.

The day of the accident was the same day as our race at Fuji Speedway. I panicked.'We've got to rush to the hospital...' I thought. Completely losing my cool, I went to bring Motoyama down from the podium. I had never prayed this much ever before; this time I really prayed… but my wish did not come true.

Daijiro had many friends beyond Road Racing world. Car drivers such as the Formula Nippon champion Satoshi Motoyama, Naoki Hattori and the Trial World Champion Takahisa Fujinami were among his best friends. *(Takashi Akamatsu)*

In 1994 Kato took part in the Suzuka Eight Hour for the first time, partnering Satoshi Tsujimoto, but crashed early in the race. *(Takashi Akamatsu)*

Satoshi Tsujimoto

Ex-All Japan racer

The end of the story called 'Daijiro Kato'

I watched Daijiro during a Honda test at Suzuka in 1994 when he stepped up to the All Japan Championship. His bike with a white fairing was rushing into the S-turn so decisively. I was surprised at how fast he was while leaning the machine, and felt he would be the only one who could be a match for Max Biaggi, who was known for his fast cornering at Grand Prix races. I wondered who he was.

Afterwards I was teamed with him for the Suzuka Eight Hour endurance race that year. I was 16 years older than him and also about 25cm taller. We got people's attention because we were an 'odd couple'. He didn't talk much but once he found his favoured setting he firmly adhered to it. Setting up the machine was soon done at his initiative. In the race Daijiro and some others plunged into bikes that had burst into flames just after the start. I visited him at the medical centre and talked to him but he didn't answer even though he hadn't got hurt: he pretended to be dead. The machine had got wrecked so we had to retire from the race. As he came back from the medical centre he said sorry in a low voice. He managed a big motorcycle so easily; he was really a great rider from the beginning.

I became so demanding of him after I became an HRC advisor. I never praised him. I must have seemed like a nagging old idiot to him. The '98 machine was not good, but what I was more worried about were the team and Daijiro, who both lost their confidence. I said to him: 'You need to study machines and tyres more.' His efforts started to pay off in 1999. 'I've found racing more interesting,' he said, and he started to stick to settings. I had an impression that he was now standing on his own feet.

Daijiro had great successes at big events, including his victory at the 1997 Japanese GP, in which he took part as a wild-card rider, followed by another win at the Japanese GP in 1998, and he took pole position at the 1997 Suzuka Eight Hour endurance race.

He displayed something special which attracted me at these races. I tried very hard to find him sponsors, to make a team for him so that he could ride on a 500cc bike at the GPs as soon as possible; I was dreaming of having a GP racing team with him. Unfortunately, I couldn't make that dream come true, but I believed he would stand on the podium at the World Championships, just like his fans expected.

Just before the accident he called me, after a long gap. 'Please come to watch my race,' he said. It was unusual for him to ask me this, so I went to Suzuka, looking forward to seeing him full of drive. I'd always got mad at him, saying, 'Try harder! You are not into the rhythm,' but I sensed that in the past year or so he was becoming more aggressive, incorporating everything into his training programme. He seemed mentally stronger. I was going to go to some tricky tracks like Assen, Catalunya and Mugello to spur him on in 2003, which was supposed to be a crucial year in his racing career.

Every time I saw him Daijiro asked me to hang out. I was presumptuous enough to tell him to do this or that, but actually there were a lot of things I learned from him. I valued him. He loved his friends and family, and that's why everyone loved him. He was very proud of his own way of life and only said what he needed to say. He was a real man. If he had got older he would have been the sort of old man young guys might be scared of.

We were all looking forward to seeing how the story called 'Daijiro Kato' would end, whether he would get to the top or not. And yet he died in a mysterious way. It was as if the curtain came down halfway through a movie that every fan of Daijiro's was enjoying. For the sake of his fans, as well as for Daijiro, we should keep trying to solve the mystery.

Daijiro teaching two-year-old Ikko how to ride a pocket bike. *(Daijiro.net)*

OPPOSITE TOP: At Suzuka, in the latter part of 2002. *From left* Shinichi Ito, Makoto Tamada, Daijiro and Tady Okada sitting in the grandstand. *(Daijiro.net)*

OPPOSITE BOTTOM: Sardinia, summer '02: Daijiro and his family holidayed on the island with Junko Yamashita and her husband. *(Daijiro.net)*

Junko Yamashita

Daijiro's team co-ordinator

He was trying to accept and respond to everything

I worked for the Shoei helmet GP racing service, so I supported Dai-chan from the time he came over to GPs, and then I began to be his co-ordinator from the middle of 2001. Normally at GPs, a rider has a manager or co-ordinator to arrange things with sponsors, the media and contracted suppliers. Special fittings, for things like leathers and boots, were a very important part of my job.

Dai-chan was very precise about his boots, as he considered feet to be very important – boots were part of the body for him, conveying the same important information as the five physical senses. He never compromised about his boots. He cared about the material and even how they were sewn. I think that showed the sensitive part of Dai-chan's personality. Alpinestars did their very best to meet Dai-chan's requests. He did not want to crash because of any mistakes changing gear.

In interviews with journalists, I would ask them to spend at least an hour to get to know him well, to avoid misunderstandings. If they spent sufficient time, building up a relationship of mutual trust, Dai-chan could respond properly. There was a time when he was asked a quick question by a journalist about 'Who is your best friend in the paddock?' But he was the kind of person who would start to think what a 'best friend' really means and eventually he got confused and could not come up with an answer. Because of that, an article was written saying that 'he has no friends', which was a bit embarrassing.

At the beginning of 2000, Team Gresini did not yet know how talented Dai-chan was, but I think that the team and Dai-chan got closer and closer after every race. Italian conversations are surprisingly long. We would go out for dinner at a restaurant at around 8 pm. Dai-chan would try to join in the conversation at the beginning of dinner but later the Italians would carry on talking among themselves. It was after midnight before they finished talking, but Dai-chan never broke into the middle of their conversation to say, 'Let's go back to hotel.' He always stuck around until the end. He didn't get cross and was patient as long as everybody else was happy.

At Malaysia, in 2002, he and the chief mechanic were in the team office for two hours. It was a one-sided talk by Fabrizio Cecchini (Dai-chan's chief mechanic) and Dai-chan kept quiet, but listened to him very seriously. He was considerate of people who were doing their best for him, so a sense of solidarity and a feeling of trust were generated naturally in the team.

Fausto Gresini and Fabrizio thought of Dai-chan like a son. He was the sort of person who made people feel 'He needs me' or 'I should help him'. Perhaps he was able to do things for himself, but the people gathered around him had the illusion that he could not do things without their help. I was one of them too.

When he finished in the top three, he did not come back to the pits as he needed to go straight away to TV interviews and the press conference. But when he did not get on the podium, he came back to the pit. I can never forget the disappointed and shamed expression on his face as he wandered around the pit putting away his boots and helmets.

There are boring times for riders during race week, such as Wednesdays or Thursdays. Everybody else is busy working and riders do not know what to do. Dai-chan was lucky because he had a wonderful family to spend time with. I think that he married his ideal woman. His wife was not the typical sort of woman who is a rider's wife, giving full support, but she did give him the sense of an ordinary life.

I recommended to Dai-chan that he should have some kind of hobby for the off days, because all he knew was racing. He began to ride bicycles and enjoy snowboarding. He seemed to be interested in scuba diving, too. In the summer of 2002, my husband and I went to Sardinia with Dai-chan's family, for a vacation. Usually Dai-chan did not clearly voice his likes or dislikes, but this time was an exception. He said, 'Let's come here again next year too!', and he swam in the sea from early morning and played with Ikko.

I will never forget that transparent blue sea and his smile.

Daijiro and his cousin, Chojun Kameya (*right*), celebrate together on the podium at Tsukuba in 1996. (*Chojun Kameya*)

Chojun Kameya

All Japan Championship racer and Daijiro's cousin

I dedicated my first victory to Daijiro

Daijiro's mother and my mother are sisters so we were cousins. We had always been together, ever since we were born. When he started to ride a pocket bike I was asked to do it with him because I was told two would have more fun than one. He was part of my childhood memories. When we were four or five he asked me to go and see planes with him after practising at Akigase, so we set out together on a journey in quest of planes, but we ended up finding nothing. As it was getting dark we became scared and went back to Akigase where the adults were in a turmoil, thinking us lost and in fear that we might have been kidnapped. They almost went to the police. We both got a big smack, and were terribly scolded. Our disappearance is still remembered by everyone as a big deal.

During the mini bike time our Akigase fellow riders organised a team and kept winning every endurance race. It was a lot of fun to spend time with them all. But I had never beaten Daijiro: he was my goal as well as my rival. Until we went to high school we were always together, studying, going for a swim or whatever. He could hardly stand being alone so always asked me to go with him.

What I remember best of the races we both took part in is the 1996 All Japan 250 Tsukuba round, where Daijiro took a win and I finished third. After taking the chequered flag I found myself running towards him to shake hands. I was very happy because it was my first podium finish, and with him on the rostrum as well. After that I left the Suzuki works team and became a privateer. When I had difficulty fundraising he supported me financially and mentally. 'You will score a win, Jun,' he always said.

It was at the Tsukuba round in 2003, after Daijiro's death, that I finally won a race. During the race I had mixed feelings, a great sense of loss, despite having strongly believed in his recovery. I was also aware of my disastrous result the previous year, when I was in 13th place. But I concentrated on training much more than usual, because I had told him I was going to quit racing if I failed in 2003. More than anything else, I swore to myself to do well in the race so that I could be proud of my riding for him. I sewed a number 74 badge on my racing suit, and put a 74 sticker on both my helmet and my machine, hoping to have Daijiro racing along with me.

I concentrated so hard on the race that I didn't hear any sounds. I was able to build up my pace from the beginning. Although the race was interrupted by a red flag I was leading the field so my concentration did not waver in the second heat, and I took my first victory after eight years in the All Japan Championship. Our Akigase fellow riders came along to cheer me for this race and they were all extremely excited. During the winning run I raised my arm into the air. 'I've won at last!' I said to Daijiro. Suddenly I remembered shaking hands with him in 1996, and then memories of Daijiro came back to me one after another. I had been forcing myself not to cry, but tears now welled up. I couldn't stop crying.

After he started seeing Maki (his wife) he became much kinder and nicer. He looked cooler and more laid back as well.

I got married when I was 20 and my eldest son Hayato is now six years old. Just four months after Daijiro's first child Ikko was born my second child Riku was born. Daijiro and I were also born in the same year, just four months apart, so I was very glad and hoped they would grow up like us. I am going to spend the rest of my life keeping in mind that I have four children, including Ikko and Rinka. I will have to try hard to become a dependable uncle for them.

Daijiro took part in the Suzuka Eight Hour in 1997 and '98 with his friend Yuichi Takeda. *(Takashi Akamatsu)*

Yuichi Takeda

Rider and driver

His last e-mail Said, 'Let's all do our best'

Daijiro and I had been very close since childhood, we were always together, so I got homesick when I went to Europe at the age of 17 to run in the Thunder Bike Championship and called him collect. 'He said, "No, thank you,"' the operator said. I didn't understand what that meant and the line went dead before I could say something. I got more depressed, and then he called me, laughing. That's just how he was.

From 1996, when I came back from Europe, to 2000, when Daijiro stepped up to the GPs, we were always together, travelling for the All Japan Championship, staying at the same hotels and having meals together. We went to Saipan with Satoshi Motoyama for training, but we didn't have much money. All we had only added up to about 5000 yen and we stayed there depending entirely on Satoshi's credit card.

'She's so cute,' he said, with heart-shaped eyes, when Daijiro met Maki (his wife). He must have fallen in love with her at first sight. 'What should I say to ask her out?' he asked me by e-mail, and I replied 'Why don't you just ask her?' His childishness seemed funny. I used to keep him company when he went out with her, but when he asked me to go to her place with him for dinner I was sensible enough not to go. 'Hey, why don't you come along?' he'd asked, quite seriously. 'I've got to tell you something,' he said later, when he told us he was marrying her. He was so embarrassed that we were embarrassed too. I was glad and happy for him, as I knew how much he loved her.

In 2003 he seemed much more committed to training, incorporating dirt track into his training programme, for example. I was against the idea of him doing dirt track because he was fast enough without drifting, and I feared his beautiful riding style might be lost. He was trying very hard, though.

When we went to a sushi restaurant in Ebisu, just before the Japanese GP, he drove into a love hotel's parking lot by mistake. 'No way!' We laughed at this a lot. 'In the past the most we could afford was a casual restaurant, but we've now grown and are able to afford sushi,' we said to each other. We talked about the Daijiro Cup over sushi. 'I want to make an original pocket bike,' he said, and we promised we would all work together to revitalise motorcycle racing and make it the way it was when we started riding. Both of us thought we had a lot of time and believed we could do anything.

Over the Japanese GP weekend I went to watch round 2 of Formula Nippon, as I had just switched to car racing. On hearing about his accident I drove from Fuji to Yokkaichi with Satoshi and Naoki Hattori in the car. I remember I felt sick with fear but I don't remember how I made it to the hospital. When I saw him hooked up to a lot of medical equipment I felt like screaming and crying, but I forced myself not to do so in front of Maki, who managed to stay calm. When she spoke to him the pointers of the equipment moved. He was striving very hard to survive.

The last e-mail from Daijiro had said, 'Let's all do our best.' That would be just like him to say that, wouldn't it? The bottom line was not Daijiro, but all of us: I guess he was trying to keep everyone together and to inspire us. Thanks to Daijiro I feel we've become strongly united. I am still suffering and sad, and I have not been able to cope with it, but I think we have to do our best.

Enjoying a barbecue on holiday. *From left* Junko Yamashita, the team co-ordinator, mechanic Ryoichi Mori, Daijiro and Haruchika Aoki, Daijiro's friend and the former 125cc World Champion. *(Makiko Kato)*

Daijiro and Satoshi Motoyama, the Formula Japan Champion, lived in the same block of flats facing the Rainbow Bridge. *(Racing on /Hiroyuki Orihara)*

Christmas party, 2002: Katsuaki Fujiwara, sitting next to Daijiro, was also a good friend. *(Makiko Kato)*

The monument to Daijiro at Autopolis circuit in Kyushu. *From left* Hiroshi Aoyama, Chojun Kameya, Tatsuya Yamaguchi, Hitoyasu Izutsu and trainer Takashi Kamata. *(Hiromi Sato)*

Satoshi Motoyama

All Japan GT and Formula Nippon Championship driver

A challenge to the world

'I've heard Daijiro was taken to hospital by helicopter, is he all right?' a guy asked me as I came out of the pit and started to walk to the starting grid for round 2 of Formula Nippon at Fuji. I wondered if he'd broken some bones or something, and went to speak to Yuichi Takeda, who was talking with somebody on the phone. When I called out to him he looked frightened. I figured then it was a serious accident and we needed to finish the race as soon as possible, to take the chequered flag quickly.

After several laps, when I'd got to the front of the field, a strange feeling hit me and I thought Daijiro might have been killed. We rushed to the hospital in Yokkaichi after the race. On the way there Yuichi and Naoki Hattori were weeping too, I guess. He was lying in the ICU but he was breathing and his hands were warm. I was so glad to find him alive.

I spent as much time as possible with him for two weeks. I was deeply worried to hear that he was struggling with the pain. 'Wouldn't it be cruel for him to be like this always?' I wondered, but I still hoped he would live. If all of us prayed a miracle might happen, so I kept saying to myself, 'We can't give up hope.' We set up a 24-hour shift so that somebody would always be with him. On the day when he looked stable and I left for Tokyo his condition suddenly changed.

It was very painful for me to race just after his passing, but due to the committed support of Kazuyoshi Hoshino, the team owner, and the team staff I won. Obviously Daijiro must have been cheering me. In 2003 I finally realised my long-standing wish and took the All Japan GT Championship title as well as the Formula Nippon Championship. Maybe I couldn't have done it without him.

We enjoyed racing together in our childhood, but I became lonely when I started karting and wasn't able to race with him any more. He was like my younger brother, and at the same time he was my rival in many ways. I was working very hard not to fall behind him in race results, income or whatever, but Daijiro had been earning contract money since he stepped up to the All Japan Championship. He was way ahead of me. I wanted to catch up with him soon, but at that time I used to run poor races where I couldn't fully show my potential. In 1998, when I went to cheer him on at the Japanese GP, where he was running as a wild card, I was greatly inspired by his efforts. He displayed overwhelming strength with a machine that was said to be not good enough for World Championships. I was mortified at my own efforts in comparison.

That experience stirred me up, as I now had a clear target: Daijiro. I took the Formula Nippon Championship title for the first time in 1998, and I felt that changed our relationship and put us on even ground – we worried about Jun or Yuichi together, for example, although Daijiro was younger.

We always checked each other's race results. When I won he asked me to treat him, and when I lost he said to me, 'That's not so cool,' by e-mail. We were neighbours as well, living in the same apartment house, on the same floor, with the same layout of rooms. During the off season in 2003 we went to Saipan for training, along with our families. I can't forget the extraordinary enthusiasm he showed there. I am now becoming keen to race overseas, as he did. I want to work hard in order to grasp what he was trying to do.

For 26 years his life seemed a very happy one, because he was loved by everyone in the world, got married to his beloved lady, and lived his life to its fullest.

In '99 Daijiro was back on form and all set to step up to the GPs.
(Takashi Akamatsu)

Makiko Kato

Daijiro's wife

There are lots of happy memories

I was pregnant in spring 2003, and I hoped to give birth when Dai-chan was in Japan. My wish came true. Yes, my new-born baby would hear his voice. She was born on 26 March, just before the Japanese GP. Dai-chan was so happy about the birth of our first girl. He said, 'I am going to steal the first kiss' and he kissed her, and I was smiling and looking at him while he was doing it.

I had one idea for her name – 'Marin' – while Dai-chan suggested another, 'Haruka'. Then we talked about how we could combine them and decided on 'Rinka'. We were planning to register her name after the race was over. He left for Suzuka, for the race, after cleaning up our house, which he rarely did, because I was weak from childbirth.

Dai-chan's parents and our son, Ikko, went to Suzuka with him but I stayed at home and watched his race on the TV with our new baby in my arms. I felt uneasy about him after I saw the pictures of the helicopter, but no one called me from the circuit so I thought he was OK. Then I changed my mind and I called his manager and asked, 'Should I come?' 'I will call you a little later,' he said, but shortly I got a call: 'Please come.' Miyo-chan (Haruchika Aoki's wife) and my elder sister kindly said, 'We can go with you', but I replied: 'I am fine.' Then I got on the Shinkansen (bullet train) alone, but on the way to the hospital I was very worried. Normally I do not eat junk food and snacks, but for some reason I was constantly eating that kind of thing on the Shinkansen. Anyone looking at me would have thought I was mad.

At the hospital I realised his condition was worse than I had imagined, but I did not believe he would die, or leave me and the kids. I thought that he would eventually recover. I truly believed it, and that's why I was OK and did not cry.

I kept on calling out to my husband, encouraging him to fight, while sitting next to him in the ICU. I said: 'You're gonna be fine! Don't give up!' All our family and friends stayed at the hotel in Yokkaichi and took turns to nurse him. One day I asked to change my turn from the morning to night because I had a bad headache. I was not usually there in the evenings, but that night I was. It was then that his condition suddenly changed for the worse.

I was remembering when we met for the first time, at a party. My first impression of him was, 'Wow, such a small face!' and that he was not my type. I never thought that we would eventually be married. After that party, he would come to pick me up after work to take me home. Sometimes he would ask me out for dinner but we were always joined by his friend, Yuichi Takeda. I thought they were kind of a pair. It was never just the two of us on a date, his friend would join us every time.

I was just an ordinary girl working in an office. I did not know anything about racing, so when I went to see my first race I was very surprised to discover such a world existed. Dai-chan was small but once he got on a bike he looked big and groovy! When he decided to go to the World Championship, he asked me to join him. It was a very big thing for me to decide: I could not follow him in a half-hearted way. I told him I needed my parents' approval, and Dai-chan came to see them. It was the tensest day of his life, asking for my parents' permission, even more so than racing.

The year 2000 was my first GP season. All the people around him were very kind to me, so I never felt out of place. Although my friends were envious of our 'international' life, in fact we stayed out in the countryside, where the races took place, and lived a simple existence. Our house in Italy was near a yacht harbour that was very lively and filled with people over the summer, but it was very quiet in the off season. The races were very exciting but our daily life in Europe was peaceful.

Ikko was born at the end of that year, and we became a family. Dai-chan was pleased by the birth of our first son and sent e-mails with a photo of the baby to all our friends. The next year, 2001, was the year that one of his dreams, of becoming a champion, came true. My dream of wearing a wedding dress at our marriage also came true at the end of that year. We were touched by the many people who came and we were very happy that day.

Dai-chan always acted naturally whether he won or lost. I would only go to the pit on race days, not on the other days, and I did not even check his qualifying results. I would treat him the same whether he performed well or not. I wanted only for him to be a good father to our children and a kind husband to me. It was never about being a champion with the greatest number of wins…

When Dai-chan went abroad for testing he would leave our son with me in Japan. Even now I feel as if he is still away on a long test. He is always on my mind, and now I feel he is closer to me than before. I feel he is really protecting me.

I remember that I was always very happy with him. There was only one time we had a fight and I was angry and cried. It is strange to say it, but even this memory is beautiful and now I feel that that day was special too. I am sure Dai-chan worries about the kids, so I have to be a good mother to stop him worrying. One thing I know for sure is that it is really good that I have children. Because of them, I strive to do my best.

Daijiro and Makiko got married on 23 December 2001. *(Makiko Kato)*

At Kauai Island in '02 Ikko tries to imitate his dad. *(Makiko Kato)*

OPPOSITE TOP: Their way of sleeping was the same… *(Makiko Kato)*

OPPOSITE BOTTOM: Ikko enjoys a game with Daijiro in '01. *(Makiko Kato)*

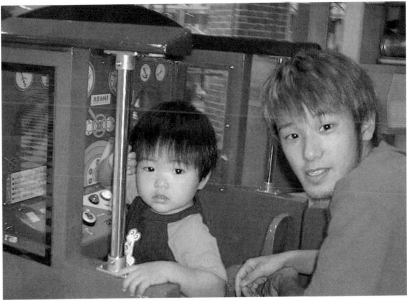

Daijiro on holiday with his family in 2002. *(Makiko Kato)*

Kauai, 2002. *(Makiko Kato)*

The photo used for the Kato family New Year card in 2003. *(Makiko Kato)*

OPPOSITE TOP: Makiko's wedding dress was made in Italy. *(Makiko Kato)*

OPPOSITE BOTTOM: Ikko joined in the wedding ceremony. *(Makiko Kato)*

Daijiro holds his second child, Rinka, before leaving for the Japanese GP in April '03. *(Makiko Kato)*

Daijiro and Makiko were a fairytale couple. At Miracosta Hotel in Tokyo Disneyland. *(Makiko Kato)*

Daijiro teaching Ikko how to swim.
(Makiko Kato)

Hiromi Sato

Motorcycle journalist

Dai-chan

It was the TBC Big Road Race in 1982 when I watched a motorcycle race for the first time, and then in 1983 I went backpacking to watch Grand Prix races in Europe. Since then I have had the opportunity to meet a lot of champion riders in person. They all have something dignified about them, the lonely aura of champions, and they are strong characters, all of which makes them look forbidding and scary. There is something different, something undeniably outstanding about them, but Dai-chan's charm altered these images I had of World Champions.

How great it was that he could bounce up to the top at his debut in the 1994 All Japan Championship, despite the disadvantages of his youth and a poorly performing machine! He was undoubtedly a rider of genius. I was completely knocked out by the gap between his overwhelming prowess on the track and the childishness he showed in the pits. As he was a high school racer in the spotlight I used to try to get comments from him, but the conversation always finished quickly. 'Dai-chan, only three lines today. Just talk for at least one page!' I would say in a friendly way, and show him my notebook, but he just chuckled and his smile made me smile as well. When he lost I wondered what was wrong with the machine or if there was a mistake in choosing tyres; I never thought it was his fault.

'He's grown up enough to give a speech,' I said to his mother, as we watched him on the podium giving an interview after his psychological battle with Shinya Nakano at Motegi, in his first Grand Prix championship outing of 2000. I said the same thing to him. 'Is that all you wanna say, instead of praising me for my victory?' he asked, but there seemed no sense praising him for that, as I took his win for granted. I found myself cheering him as if I were his aunt.

I was glad when Dai-chan started seeing Maki (his wife). He loved her very much, and that made him very happy. I e-mailed him to say 'Congratulations' on winning the 2001 World Championship. 'I hardly noticed it because I'm still busy taking care of Ikko (his son) and nothing has changed,' he replied. 'You are very dear to your family whether you are a world champion or not,' I emailed back. 'Maki tells me she would dump me if I didn't look out for my family,' he bragged, when I saw him afterwards.

Dai-chan was so straightforward: I wanna win as it's a race; I wanna be top as it's a competition; I wanna stay together because I love her; I'm gonna get married as we're having a baby. He was simple, and decisive, and a good sport in every way. He even began to be able to fill my notebook, and to think about the future of motorsport – thinking of a never-ending future, he was trying to leave something behind. He changed from a boy who was so cute and childish that I felt like stroking his head to Daijiro Kato, able to stand firmly on his own feet.

I still just cannot accept his passing. I am shocked to find how deeply I wished for his success and looked forward to seeing him smiling happily. I almost begin to cry when I see his mother, but I have not had a good cry yet. I asked Maki if she had been able to have a good cry. 'That's a secret, and I am not the type to cry in public,' she smiled sadly. It might take forever to fill a Daijiro-shaped hollow that gapes in everyone's heart, but I hope to cry my fill someday.

Japanese GP, 2003: Daijiro was aiming for the World Championship that year. *(Takashi Akamatsu)*

Yoko Togashi

Motorcycle journalist

The wind in Estoril

More than twenty years ago, I lost my friends Kazuyuki Ishide and Iwao Ishikawa at racetracks. They were both close friends of mine and we would go on vacation trips during the off season along with many other racing friends. Also, I was teaching English to Ishikawa when he decided to take part in GPs in 1983. I shared his dream of becoming a World Champion.

After they passed away I tried to put some distance between Japanese racers and myself. I have to work with them for my job as a motorcycle journalist, but I decided it would go no further. This was because the deaths of Ishikawa and Ishide were so devastating that I could not contemplate the sadness of losing any more friends.

I guess I was trying to put a transparent barrier in front of me so that no more Japanese riders could approach me, but Daijiro just stepped over the barrier so easily that I did not realise he was there.

When HRC decided to take Daijiro to GPs, I started to teach him English. He knew that he would have to communicate in English with his team staff and the media when he joined a European team, so he was desperate to learn the language.

I made a question and answer sheet and got Daijiro to reply to hypothetical questions. One day I asked him, 'Which racetrack do you like best?' and he answered, 'Suzuka.' 'Why?' I continued, but there was no answer. He looked like he was thinking. I expected answers such as 'Because it is a technical course' or 'Because it is a high-speed track and I like high-speed tracks', and thought that perhaps he couldn't express his feelings in English.

I said to him, 'You can tell me in Japanese and I will translate it for you.' Daijiro answered, 'I can't explain in Japanese either…' He was trying to understand why he liked Suzuka but he could not understand the reason himself. Then I realised: genius is like this. If a genius can perform well in his special area, he doesn't have to express his feelings verbally. In other words, if he is good at what he does, it is not necessary for him to become a spokesman.

In 2000, when Daijiro started to take part in GPs as a regular rider, I went to Europe twice to see his races. When I was there, there was tacit consent that I would do all the translation for his TV interviews and press conferences. (When I was not there, a person from NHK, the Japanese national broadcasting station, did the job instead of me.)

When Daijiro finished third in Mugello, in Italy, I could not get near him after the race, as guards were stopping us from getting into the parc fermé area. A TV interview was due in a short while and, if I couldn't get to him, Daijiro would have to do the interview on his own. Daijiro was searching for me, and he looked nervous and fragile. Finally, I escaped from the guard and reached him: his face lit up and he looked so relieved. That was when my transparent barrier collapsed.

I was still concerned that Daijiro would never speak English during the press conferences, even if I helped him all the time. Other Japanese riders would speak either English or Italian and were able to express their feelings without the aid of a translator.

Then at Estoril, in Portugal, in September 2000, I told Daijiro after the final qualifying session, 'From now on, you must speak in English during the press conference, or you never will.' He said, 'Oh, no!' and his face became pale. He looked so lonely and sad that I said, 'If you win here, I will do the translation for you. So try your best!' Daijiro just said, 'Yes, I will.'

Daijiro had not won a race that year since the opening round at Suzuka, in April, so perhaps I was thinking it was impossible for him to win at Estoril. However, he won the race the next day. I was really happy and excited while I waited in front of the TV interview room for Daijiro to return from the cooling-down lap. When he came back and found me, he said happily, 'I won!' After that, whenever I was at European racetracks, I did the translations for Daijiro.

After Daijiro died there was a big hole in my heart, with a sad wind blowing through it. I remember a strong wind was blowing at Estoril, the wind from the Atlantic Ocean…

Daijiro on the morning of the Japanese GP, 2003. *(Team Gresini)*

Words from Daijiro

'I didn't know that Harada-san was going to retire. But I was lucky to have a chance to race against him.'
When he was asked, 'What did you think at the Valencia GP in '02 when you heard that Harada was going to retire?'

'Because he has won the World Championship.'
When asked, 'Do you think Valentino Rossi is a good rider? If so, why?'

'I feel better at GPs than at the All Japan Championship, because at the All Japan Championship races everybody speaks Japanese and there are many people whom I know, but in GPs I don't have to worry about anything.'
When asked, 'Which is more comfortable for you, the All Japan Championship or the GPs?'

'My hero was Kevin Schwantz. I first saw a motorcycle race video when I was a kid. That was when Freddie Spencer was still racing. My dad bought videos and made me watch them.'
When asked, 'Who was your hero when you were a kid?'

'It was a bit weird to hear him praising me like that.'
When asked, 'Have you read the article where Makoto Tamada praised your riding as ideal and perfect?'

'Of course, sometimes I get fired up and excited. But after a few laps, I become ashamed of myself for getting too excited.'
When told, 'You always look cool and as though you are thinking about tactics during the race.'

'You don't want to lose at anything, do you, for instance, in card games or playing TV games. I hate losing.'
When told, 'You seem to hate being second best.'

'I know it wouldn't be easy, but I would still try.'
When asked, 'Would you accept a challenge at a sport other than motorcycle racing?'

'Of course we are racing in order to win, so we cannot always be fair and gentleman-like. But I don't like winning by bumping into other riders and so forth.'
When asked, 'Tetsuya Harada said you are fair and ride cleanly. What do you think?'

'Oh, yes?'
When told, 'Your girlfriend Maki is cute and charming' before their marriage.

'If he wants to, I don't mind him riding a motorcycle for fun. Maybe it would be nice if we could play with it together.'
When asked, 'What will you do if Ikko wants to ride a motorcycle in the future?'

'I hear that racing is less popular nowadays in Japan, so I hope there will be more kids enjoying motorcycle racing soon. I was brought up at Akigase so I started the Daijiro Cup from there. I hope one day there will be more kids racing motorcycles.'
When asked about the Daijiro Cup (a pocket bike championship series).

'I will take this year's Japanese GP not as one of the sixteen GPs, but like a race in the old days, when I was taking part as a wild-card rider. I mean, I will treat it as an important race in which I only take part once a year.'
When asked, 'What is your hope for this race, the 2003 Japanese GP?'

'I don't feel comfortable there. It's so strange. But I must get used to it.'
When asked at Suzuka '03, 'What is your impression of the new chicane?'

'She has a small face and resembles me more than Ikko. She should have resembled Maki, 'cos she is a girl.'
When asked, 'How is your new baby? She is sweet, isn't she?' on 3 April 2003 at Suzuka. His answer sounded modest, but he looked very happy.

'Rin Rin sounds nice, doesn't it?'
When he was thinking of Rinka's name at Suzuka.

Epilogue

Hope

On 6 April 2003 the cherry trees were shedding their blossom in the strong wind. The helicopter with Dai-chan on board took off as if it were being sucked into the blue sky. At the hospital in Yokkaichi, where he was taken, meeting rooms were opened up for the many people who had rushed there, but after visiting hours were over everyone was told to go home. No one would leave, however, and I spent the night with them outside the hospital, shivering with cold and fear. A shooting star glittered, changing from orange to blue as I looked silently up at the sky. Everyone's eyes were glued to it as well. I wished hard upon it, so hard that my clenched hands grew pale. It was the same for everyone. I wondered how many fans of Dai-chan were wishing the same thing, around the world.

There was a clear blue sky for both the wake service and the funeral. At the memorial service, held forty-nine days after Dai-chan's passing, a large rainbow appeared in the blue sky after the rain had stopped. It came close to disappearing and then the colours became deeper and more beautiful. 'Maybe Daijiro went up to heaven by crossing over the rainbow,' said Takashi Kato, his father, staring at it.

After that he left for Italy. I heard that the passenger gate in France, for the connecting flight, was 74D. Daijiro was very popular in Europe. A 'Via Daijiro' was built on the road linking Misano circuit to the national highway. Mr Kato and his companions paid a courtesy visit to the Mayor of Misano, and then bade farewell to Italy. On the beautiful slope overlooking the track, which is closely connected with Dai-chan, a '74' monument has been built to commemorate his achievements by volunteers who asked for contributions by word of mouth.

A lot of people have visited Dai-chan's house since his passing. Makiko never misses a day without offering flowers in front of his picture, so he is always surrounded by beautiful blooms and is smiling like a hero in girls' comics. On 4

July a lot of people gathered at his house to celebrate his twenty-seventh birthday, putting pictures of him all over the walls, blowing up a lot of balloons in his team colours of yellow, blue and white, and enjoying good food and a great big cake. Everyone who was there felt sorrow at Daijiro's absence, for he was supposed to be there too, the life and soul of the party, but they made merry to forget their grief.

I believe all his friends and fans throughout the world have him in their minds constantly, and not a day passes when they don't remember him. They are probably looking for answers from Daijiro: 'Would he do it this way?' or 'How would he feel in this case?' Dai-chan, who is now able to fly anywhere, like an angel, must be very busy.

I think every one of them is also trying to pay respect to the memories he left behind and the kind feelings they became aware of through him. They are also trying very hard to make their own dreams come true – Daijiro would not feel happy if somebody felt sadness because of him. I hope this book will be an acceptable offering for fans like this.

The idea for the book came from a conversation I had with Yoko Togashi, a lady whom I admire and respect. Both of us wanted to put together something that would help his children understand their father when, one day, they begin to wonder what he was like. If it can also provide you with some hints about why he was called a genius and was loved by everybody, I couldn't be happier. I would like to thank the 74 people who agreed to our interviews, the photographers who provided us with pictures, Shinichi Fukushima at Kodansya Ltd, who was patient enough to accommodate our many requests, and all Daijiro's family members. And to you, who have picked up this book, I am of course very grateful.

Hiromi Sato

Results

1993

1. Kyushu Road Race Championship
Team Kotake with RSC

GP250	Honda RS250R
GP125	Honda RS125R
SP250	Honda NSR250R

Date	Circuit		Q	R
21/3	HRS Kyushu	GP2500	1	1
		GP125	2	1
11/4	HRS Kyushu	SP250	1	1
9/5	HRS Kyushu	GP250	1	1
		GP125	1	1
30/5	Aso RP	GP250	2	1
		SP250	1	1
20/6	HRS Kyushu	SP250	1	1
1/8	HRS Kyushu	SP250	2	1
12/9	HRS Kyushu	GP250	1	1
		GP125	1	1
17/10	SPA Naoiri	GP250	1	1
		GP125	1	1
31/10	HRS Kyushu	SP250	2	1
14/11	Aso RP	GP125	1	1
28/11	HRS Kyushu	GP250	1	1
		SP250	1	1

Ranking: GP250 – 1
GP125 – 1
SP250 – 1

2. Suzuka Road Race Championship
Team Kotake with RSC

| SP250 | Honda NSR250R |

Date	Q	R
4/4	1	2
13/6	4	DNF
24/7	3	6
5/12	1	1

Ranking: 6

3. Kanto Road Race Championship
Team 1 Factory

| SP250 | Honda RS250R |
| SP250 | Honda NSR250R |

Date	Circuit		Q	R
21/2	TSUKUBA	SP250	2	1
		GP250	1	1
23/5	TSUKUBA	GP250	1	DNF
11/7		GP250	1	1
26/9	TSUKUBA	GP250	1	DNF
24/10	TSUKUBA	GP250	1	1

Ranking: GP250 – 3
SP250 – 15

1994

All Japan Road Race Championship
Team Kotake with RSC

| GP250 | Honda RS250R |

Date	Circuit	Q	R
13/3	SUZUKA	2	DNF
10/4	MINE	1	25
1/5	SUGO	4	26
15/5	TSUKUBA	5	2
29/5	FUJI	2	4
12/6	SUZUKA	1	28
3/7	SUGO	9	3
11/9	SUZUKA	4	4
25/9	T I Aida	3	1
9/10	SUGO	1	3
30/10	TSUKUBA	14	DNF

Ranking: 7

1995

All Japan Road Race Championship
Team Kotake with RSC

| GP250 | Honda RS250R |

Date	Circuit	Q	R
30/4	SUGO	3	4
14/5	TUKUBA	1	DNF
28/5	FUJI	3	4
11/6	SUZUKA	1	31
2/7	SUGO	2	35
20/8	MINE	1	1
10/9	SUZUKA	2	1
1/10	T I Aida	1	8
22/10	SUGO	6	8
12/11	SUZUKA	7	8

Ranking: 5

(Takashi Akamatsu)

(Takashi Akamatsu)

1996

All Japan Road Race Championship
Team Kotake with RSC

GP250   Honda NSR250

Date	Circuit	Q	R
17/3	SUZUKA	4	7
28/4	SUGO	1	1
19/5	TUKUBA	1	1
9/6	SUZUKA	4	4
23/6	FUJI	6	1
7/7	SUGO	1	18
11/8	MINE	1	2
8/9	SUZUKA	5	DNF
22/9	TUKUBA	2	Cancelled
6/10	T I Aida	1	1
3/11	SUGO	5	2

Ranking: 2

Wild Card – 1996 Japanese GP

21/4	SUZUKA GP250	5	2

1997

All Japan Road Race Championship
Castrol Honda (HRC)

GP250   Honda NSR250

Date	Circuit	Q	R
16/3	SUZUKA	DNS	DNS
27/4	SUGO	1	1
18/5	TUKUBA	1	1
1/6	SUZUKA	3	1
22/6	FUJI	1	1
6/7	SUGO	3	3
10/8	MINE	1	3
7/9	SUZUKA	1	1
21/9	TUKUBA	1	1
19/10	T I Aida	1	1
2/11	SUGO	5	1

Ranking: 1

Wild Card – 1997 Japanese GP

20/4	SUZUKA GP250	3	1

1998

All Japan Road Race Championship
Castrol Honda (HRC)

GP250   Honda NSR250

Date	Circuit	Q	R
12/4	MOTEGI	2	2
26/4	SUGO	12	5
17/5	TUKUBA	4	DNF
31/5	SUZUKA	3	2
9/8	MINE	2	DNF
6/9	TUKUBA	3	DNF
20/9	SUZUKA	4	3
18/10	TUKUBA	DNS	DNS
1/11	SUGO	DNS	DNS

Ranking: 8

Wild Card – 1998 Japanese GP

5/4	SUZUKA GP250	1	1

1999

All Japan Road Race Championship
Castrol Honda (HRC)

GP250   Honda NSR250

Date	Circuit	Q	R
21/3	MINE	3	2
2/5	SUGO	1	2
16/5	TUKUBA	2	29
30/5	SUZUKA	3	2
13/6	MOTEGI	2	1
22/8	SUGO	3	2
5/9	SUZUKA	3	1
19/9	TUKUBA	1	1
24/10	T I Aida	1	1
7/11	MOTEGI	1	1

Ranking: 2

Wild Card – 1999 Japanese GP

25/4	MOTEGI GP250	10	5

(Takashi Akamatsu)

2000

World Championship Grand Prix 250cc class
AOX Honda Gresini

Honda   NSR250

Date	Circuit	Q	R
19/3	South Africa/Welkom	3	2
4/2	Malaysia/Sepang	2	3
9/4	Japan/Suzuka	1	1
30/4	Spain/Jerez	3	2
14/5	France/Le Mans	1	6
28/5	Italy/Mugello	8	3
11/6	Catalunya	7	4
24/6	Dutch/Assen	6	8
9/7	Great Britain/Donington	5	10
23/7	Germany/Sachsenring	7	4
20/8	Czech/Brno	8	6
3/9	Portugal/Estoril	2	1
17/9	Valencia	13	5
7/10	Rio	3	1
15/10	Pacific/Motegi	1	1
29/10	Australia/Philip Island	3	3

Ranking: 3 – Rookie Of The Year

(Team Gresini)

2001

World Championship Grand Prix 250cc class
Telefonica Movister Honda Gresini

Honda   NSR250

Date	Circuit	Q	R
8/4	Japan/Suzuka	1	1
22/4	South Africa	1	1
6/5	Spain	1	1
20/5	France	1	1
3/6	Italy	6	10
17/6	Catalunya	1	1
30/6	Dutch	2	11
8/7	Great Britain	2	1
22/7	Germany	3	2
26/8	Czech	2	3
9/9	Portugal	2	1
23/9	Valencia	5	1
7/10	Pacific/Motegi	2	DNF
14/10	Australia	3	1
21/10	Malaysia	1	1
3/11	Rio	2	1

Ranking: 1

(Team Gresini)

2002

MotoGP – Fortuna Honda Gresini

MotoGP   NSR500 (1-9)
               RC211V (10-16)

Date	Circuit	Q	R
7/4	Japan/Suzuka	6	10
21/4	South Africa	14	4
5/5	Spain	4	2
19/5	France	5	DNF
2/6	Italy	16	DNF
16/6	Catalunya	15	8
29/6	Dutch	17	12
14/7	Great Britain	11	7
21/7	Germany	9	DNF
25/8	Czech	2	2
8/9	Portugal	2	DNF
21/9	Rio	6	DNF
6/10	Pacific/Motegi	1	DNF
13/10	Malaysia	3	5
20/10	Australia	10	4
3/11	Valencia	3	4

(Team Gresini)

Ranking: *7 – Rookie Of The Year*

2003

MotoGP – Telefonica Movister Honda Gresini

Honda   RC211V

Date	Circuit	Q	R	
6/4	Japan/Suzuka	11	DNF	*(Team Gresini)*

Suzuka 8-hour Endurance Race

Date	Team	Machine	Partner	Q	R
31/7/1994	Team HRC	RVF/RC45	Satoshi Tsujimoto	5	DNF
30/7/1995	Team Kotake	RSC RVF/RC45	Terry Rymer	14	12
27/7/1997	Team Kunimitsu	RVF/RC45	Yuichi Takeda	1	9
26/7/1998	Lucky Strike HSC	RVF/RC45	Yuichi Takeda	4	DNF
25/7/1999	Team Kotake with Sakurai Honda	RVF/RC45	Makoto Tamada	3	6
30/7/2000	Team Cabin Honda	VTR1000SPW	Tohru Ukawa	4	1
5/8/2001	Team Cabin Honda	VTR1000SPW	Tohru Ukawa	3	4
4/8/2002	Team Cabin Honda	VTR1000SPW	Colin Edwards	2	1

Credits and acknowledgments

Special thanks to
Makiko Nakamura
Junko Yamashita
Russell Colwell
Iain Mackay
Shinichi Fukushima (Kodansha Publishing Co Ltd)
Masato Maebayashi

All the photographers, Daijiro's family and friends

Publisher's note

The title and status of the 74 people are of those when the Japanese version was published in April 2004. When you read 'this year' within the book, it means 2003, when the interviews took place.

Yoko Togashi

Born in Tokyo.
Works as a translator, freelance journalist, Honda Motor/HRC PR advisor.
Ex-roadracer.
Travelled in South America in 1982.
Started to cover GPs in 1980.
In 1988, wrote the book *One Day We Will,* which is about the NR500 and the Freddie Spencer v. Kenny Roberts fight (in 1983).
Other books include GP Riders, *The Legend of Pops Yoshimura,* etc.

Hiromi Sato

Born in Miyagi-Prefecture.
Works as a freelance writer, editor and co-ordinator.
Started to cover GPs in 1983.
Has covered the GPs, the All Japan Championship, the Suzuka Eight Hour race, etc.
Works as a writer on the Tokyo *Chunichi* sports newspaper, covering the All Japan Championship.